# JOB MATTERS

## ELEKTROTECHNIK

von
Michael Benford
Wolf-Rainer Windisch

unter Mitarbeit der Verlagsredaktion

Cornelsen

# How to use the book

*Job Matters Elektrotechnik* wurde für die Ausbildung in Berufsschulen sowie die innerbetriebliche Aus- und Weiterbildung konzipiert und bietet Ihnen praxisorientiertes Fachenglisch basierend auf den Anforderungen des Gemeinsamen Europäischen Referenzrahmens (A2-B1).

## So finden Sie sich im Buch zurecht:

Zu Beginn jeder Unit finden Sie eine Übersicht über die Themen und sprachlichen Fertigkeiten, die in der jeweiligen Unit behandelt werden.

**IT'S YOUR TURN**

Die *It's your turn*-Aufgaben am Ende jeder Unit stellen einen zusammenfassenden Abschluss der Unit dar und richten sich an diejenigen, die gezielt an weiterführenden sprachlichen Fertigkeiten arbeiten möchten. Hier können zudem eigene Erfahrungen der Lernenden eingebracht werden.

**▶▶▶ ICH KANN**

| | Seite/Übung |
|---|---|
| ☐ Ich kann meine Meinung, Pläne, Absichten und Ziele darlegen und einfach begründen. B1 | 59/ It's your turn |

Nach jeder vierten Unit greifen *Extra practice*-Seiten das Gelernte noch einmal auf und bieten so ein zusätzliches Übungsangebot zu den Themen der vorherigen Units. Außerdem zeigen *Can-do-Statements*, welche Fertigkeiten die Lernenden in den Units erworben und gefestigt haben.

Für heterogene Klassen werden innerhalb der einzelnen Units differenzierte Aufgaben angeboten und durch Sterne gekennzeichnet (★ = niedriger Schwierigkeitsgrad, ★★ = mittlerer Schwierigkeitsgrad, ★★★ = hoher Schwierigkeitsgrad).

| | |
|---|---|
| It consists of … | The current in the … is higher/lower than the current in … |
| It is made up of … | The contacts in the … are normally open/closed. |
| The current enters the … | When the switch is thrown, the coil … |
| The current passes through the … | When the switching circuit is completed, … |
| The contactor gets its current from … | If the overload heaters trip, they … |

Praxisbezogene Redewendungen und Phrasen finden Sie in den grünen Kästen.

## Weitere wichtige Symbole:

2 = kennzeichnet Höraufgaben und gibt den entsprechenden Track an. Die Hörbeispiele sind separat als Download (ISBN 9783064513297) unter www.cornelsen.de erhältlich.

= kennzeichnet Tipps und wichtige Hinweise

Viel Spaß beim Lernen und gutes Gelingen wünschen Ihnen die Autoren und der Verlag!

# Contents

# 1 Your career

**This unit is about:**
- basic skills
- career opportunities
- activities

**Competences:**
- listening to a radio interview
- discussing career options
- describing your work

## 2 1 Starting out

Martin Müller at the German Economic Chambers talks to a BBC reporter about the training needed to become an electrician.

★ a) Listen to the interview and complete the dialogue with the words you hear.

Interviewer: What sort of person makes a good electrician?

Martin: We are looking for young people with a ________________[1] for all things electrical. We want people who love their work and want to learn more and more all the time.

Interviewer: So how much must an electrician learn?

Martin: The first training phase of the apprenticeship is a year of ________________[2] training which is the same for all jobs in the industry. After that, they specialise in a particular ________________[3] which takes two and a half years.

Interviewer: That's a long training course! Why does it last so long?

Martin: Electricity can kill, so we make sure that apprentices first have an excellent understanding of the basics. Our modern world is changing fast. What is new today will be old in six months' time, so electricians will need to keep up with these changes for the rest of their working life.

Interviewer: Yes, I understand. Could you give us some examples of basic training?

Martin: Teamwork, communication with colleagues and clients, ________________[4] and testing, tools and equipment, safety measures, understanding technical ________________[5], basic installation work, fault-finding, basic hard and software handling skills and, of course, English.

Interviewer: And the second phase?

Martin: Energy and ________________[6] technology, energy technology, systems and ________________[7] technology and ________________[8] and process control technology.

★★ b) Work with a partner and use the information in the dialogue to ask each other
- what training phase of the apprenticeship your partner is in (basic or specialist training).
- what his/her specialization was/is / will be.
- why he/she has chosen this specialization.

★★★ c) Write a few sentences about your partner. Begin like this:
*Fabian/Kerstin is ... years old. He/She ...*

______________________________________________

______________________________________________

Read it out to the class when you have finished. Are the details correct?

## 2 Specializing

Electricity workers can specialize in various fields.

★ a) Read what four apprentices say about the main phase of their apprenticeship, then match these statements with four of the six specializations in the box.

network and communications technology • planning and installing building management systems • rail electrification technology • renewable energies • security systems • servicing building management systems

Kerstin
Every day's different. Yesterday I had to climb up on the roof of a very tall building to check the photovoltaic system. Tomorrow we're installing solar panels. I love it!

______________________________

Ramazan
We install technology to make it very hard to break into a building. We often meet the people who live or work there, and some of them are very famous. It's exciting work!

______________________________

Fabian
Nowadays, you can control a building remotely with a laptop or smartphone, e.g. set the temperature, lock or unlock the doors, etc. We find out what the customer wants and install it.

______________________________

Sven
We have to work all hours because an overhead power cable can be damaged by a falling tree in a storm for example, so we come out and repair it to get the trains running again.

______________________________

★★ b) Complete the sentences with eight of the ten words in blue in the four texts above.

My company services building management systems, which means we ______________ [1] that everything is working properly. Some of the buildings also have expensive security systems because ______________ [2] people such as sports stars or TV celebrities live there. If something is ______________ [3] – an electrical switch or socket is broken, for example – I can often ______________ [4] it myself. Some building owners use their smartphones to turn up the heating and switch on the lights ______________ [5] before they arrive home. Others use a laptop to ______________ [6] the temperature and switch on the alarm system at night. Many have a ______________ [7] system because they prefer to use renewable energy sources. It's best to ______________ [8] all these special systems when the house is built and not later because retrofits are expensive!

**IT'S YOUR TURN**

Your college's website needs to be updated with an overview of all the jobs the college trains students for. Write a profile of your work as an electrician for the English section of the website. Use the language box and your own ideas.

I work for … (company) in … It has … employees and … apprentices.
I'm in the … module of my training course. It will last … years.

I have chosen … as my specialization because …

I like electrical engineering because I like installing / repairing / working on …

Later I want to work for … (company) / have my own company / study / work abroad.

# 2 What is electricity?

**This unit is about:**
- the parts of the atom
- electron flow
- natural phenomena

**Competences:**
- listening to a dialogue
- understanding special electrical terms

3 ## 1 Electricity

In this dialogue you will hear some important, basic electricity terms.

★ a) First read the dialogue with a partner and guess which words are missing. Then listen to the recording and check your answers.

Lightning: 109 volts (up to 1 gigavolt)

Trainee: What exactly is electricity?

Instructor: Well, to understand electricity you first have to understand the difference between voltage and current. Do you know anything about them?

Trainee: Well, everybody knows that the voltage in the mains is ______________[1] and current means something that flows.

Instructor: Exactly. Electricity flows along a conductor, like copper wire. To understand all this let's first look at the basic building block of all things – the atom. What are atoms made of?

Trainee: Things like protons, electrons and ________________[2]?

Instructor: Very good! Let's look at the electrons and protons. These atomic particles have an electric charge. Protons are positive and electrons are ____________[3]. They are opposites and what do you know about opposites?

A spark across spark plug terminals: about 20,000V

Trainee: Opposites attract.

Instructor: Exactly. If you separate electrons and protons, a force is produced between them because they want to get back together again. This force is called the potential ________________[4] or voltage. A voltage is a force waiting to be set free. In this case, the electrons want to get to the protons. A battery is a good example of this. How do you get power from a battery?

Trainee: You put a load between the positive and negative ________________[5].

Instructor: And so what do you think flows between the terminals?

Trainee: Electrons. OK, now I understand what current is.

Instructor: Yes, it's a flow of electrons, but to understand it in more detail, imagine that in one terminal of a battery electrons are missing. What is it now – positive or negative?

Trainee: ________________[6].

Instructor: Very good! The positive terminal has "holes" waiting for electrons. In the other terminal, the negative one, there are lots of extra electrons waiting to get to those holes. If you put a ________________[7] between the two terminals, electrons rush down it to get to the holes and on the way they can power a load, for example a light bulb. Can you think of a good conductor?

Trainee: You mentioned copper a moment ago.

Instructor: Exactly. Copper is a good conductor. Electrons flow along it easily. It has very low ________________[8]. Now let's think of different ways to separate electrons and protons …

★★ b) Use the information in the text to label the battery terminals positive or negative.

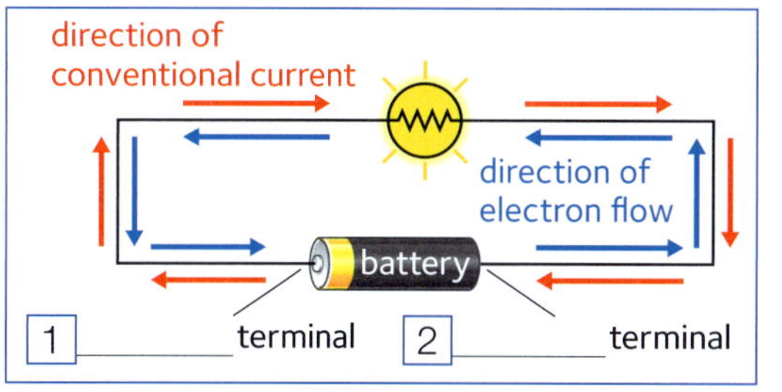


## 2 Voltage and current

It is important for electricians to know about voltage and current.

★ a) Read the text and match the words in blue with their German equivalents in the box.

Voltage[1] is the force which causes a current[2] to flow in a closed electrical circuit[3]. It is symbolized by the letters E or V and is measured[4] in volts (V). Current is a flow of charged[5] particles (e.g. electrons). The flow of the current outside the power source is from the plus terminal to the minus one. The electrons move[6] in the opposite[7] direction. The value of the current depends on[8] the number of electrons which pass a fixed point per second. Current is symbolized by the letter I and is measured in amperes or amps (A).

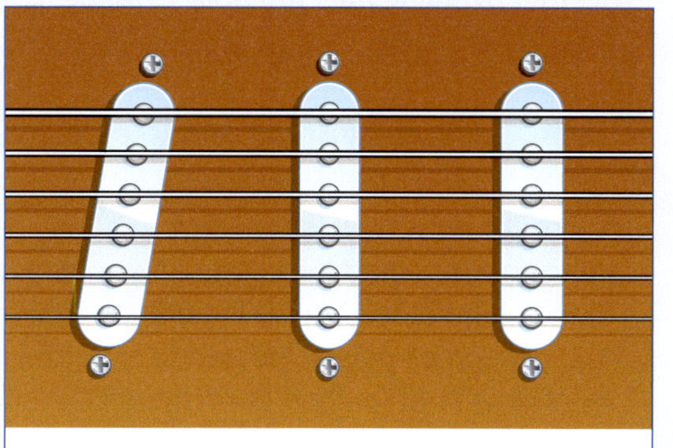

Electric guitar pickups have magnets to generate electricity.

☐ bewegen sich • ☐ entgegengesetzt • ☐ geladen • ☐ gemessen • ☐ hängt von … ab • ☐ Schaltkreis • ☐ Spannung • ☐ Strom

★★ b) Choose the right answer to complete the sentences.

1 A current a) is always a flow of electrons b) is a flow of protons c) can be a flow of anything.
2 Voltage is a measure of a) force b) resistance c) current.
3 A potential difference can exist between a) protons and neutrons b) electrons and protons c) electrons and neutrons.
4 When electrons and protons are separated, a) the electrons try to get to the protons b) the protons become neutrons c) the neutrons try to get to the protons.
5 A good conductor has a) low resistance to protons b) high resistance to electrons c) low resistance to electrons.

**Tip**

An average bolt of lightning has a current of 300–500 kiloamperes at a potential difference of up to 1 gigavolt (1 billion volts), but it lasts for only 0.0004 seconds. This is enough energy to light a 100 watt light bulb for about 45 years.

★★★ c) Fill in the gaps with words from the dialogue, the definitions and the diagram.

When you connect electrical equipment to the ____________ 1, the ____________ 2 is 230V. The metal most often used as a ____________ 3 is ____________ 4 because it has very low ____________ 5 to electrons. The flow of electrons is called the ____________ 6 and is measured in ____________ 7. Electricity is normally used to power a ____________ 8, e.g. a motor. The quantity of electrons waiting to flow is the ____________ 9 difference. It is measured in ____________ 10.

**IT'S YOUR TURN**

You want to understand more about lightning and static electricity. Work with a partner, research one of these two topics and prepare a short presentation for your class.

# 3 DC voltage: batteries

| This unit is about: | Competences: |
|---|---|
| • direct current generation | • understanding a technical text |
| • commonly used battery types | • understanding spoken instructions |
| • rechargeable batteries | • giving a technical explanation |

## 1 Dry cell batteries

This text explains how dry cell batteries work.

★ a) Read the text and then label the parts of the battery with the words in blue.

The most common source of direct current is a battery. Zinc-carbon (dry cell) batteries (e.g. AAA, AA, C and D) are the most common type of commercial battery. The cathode is a carbon rod. It is placed in the middle of a zinc casing, which forms the anode. The space around it is filled with an acid paste. When they are connected by a conductor (e.g. a copper wire), electrons from the anode (zinc) flow along the wire to the cathode (carbon) and produce a current. Whereas in a battery the anode is negative, in a device that consumes power, the anode is positive. The zinc of the anode is eaten up by the acid during this reaction and when there is no more zinc left, the battery is dead. In some batteries the chemical reaction can be reversed by an external voltage. These batteries are called rechargeable batteries or accumulators. Unfortunately, they cannot be recharged indefinitely. How often an accumulator can be recharged depends on the technology used. Car batteries using lead and lead-dioxide plates are one of the longest lasting types of accumulator.

A further source of DC voltage is photovoltaic cells. Photovoltaic cells are becoming more and more important for generating electricity.

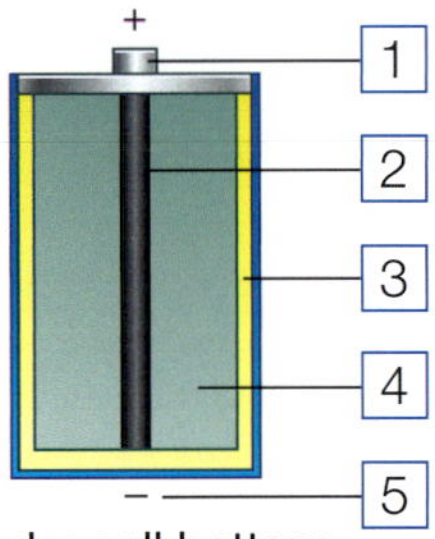


1 ____________
2 ____________
3 ____________
4 ____________
5 ____________

dry cell battery

★★ b) Study the text and the diagram and then say which five statements are false.

| | | T | F |
|---|---|---|---|
| 1 | A battery produces direct current. | | |
| 2 | The anode of a battery is positive. | | |
| 3 | The cathode is often made of carbon. | | |
| 4 | Electrons flow from the cathode to the anode. | | |
| 5 | In a zinc-carbon battery the acid paste eats up the carbon. | | |
| 6 | The zinc casing of a dry cell battery is negative. | | |
| 7 | An accumulator is a rechargeable battery. | | |
| 8 | An accumulator can't be recharged very often if it has lead and lead-dioxide plates. | | |
| 9 | A photovoltaic cell is a form of battery. | | |

★★★ c) Correct the false statements above.

1 ____________________
2 ____________________
3 ____________________
4 ____________________
5 ____________________

4

## 2 How a simple battery works

You are going to hear someone explaining how a simple battery works. Put the sentences in the right order. Start with D. Then listen to the recording and check your sentences.

A "Holes" for the missing electrons are produced in these protons. ☐

B A lead dioxide plate, which is called the cathode, is carefully put into the acid on the other side of the vessel. ☐

C A lead plate, which is called the anode, is carefully put into the acid on one side of the vessel. ☐

D A strong glass vessel is half-filled with sulphuric acid. 1

E Electricity is generated. ☐

F Electrons in the lead dioxide plate are separated from their protons by a chemical reaction. ☐

G Electrons in the lead plate are freed by the sulphuric acid. ☐

H It can be used to power a load. ☐

I The free electrons from the anode are attracted to the protons with holes in the cathode. ☐

J The two plates are connected by a copper wire. ☐

## 3 DC voltage

Complete these passive sentences with one of the following words.

connected • eaten • generated • produced • separated • used

**Tip**

They **are connected** by a wire.
The rod **is placed** in the middle.

1 Electrons are ________________ from the atoms by the acid.

2 The terminals are ________________ by a piece of copper wire.

3 Protons with missing electrons are ________________ by the chemical reaction.

4 The zinc is ________________ up by the acid.

5 Lead is ________________ by car battery manufacturers.

6 Electricity is ________________ by using photovoltaic cells.

## 4 Appliances

Do you know which appliance needs which battery? Match the appliances with the correct battery.

1 car → ________________

2 digital camera → ________________

3 smoke detector → ________________

4 torch → ________________

5 TV remote control → ________________

6 wristwatch → ________________

**Battery types**

| Voltage | Name |
|---|---|
| 12V | car battery |
| 9V | PP3 / block battery |
| 4.5V | 4.5 volt battery |
| 1.5V | D |
| 1.5V | C |
| 1.5V | AA (double A) |
| 1.5V | AAA (triple A) |
| 1.5–3V | button cell |

**IT'S YOUR TURN**

During your apprenticeship you need to explain how batteries work. With a partner, draw a diagram of one of the batteries in exercise 4 and give a short presentation.

# 4 AC voltage sources: dynamos and generators

**This unit is about:**
- how alternating current is generated
- the direction in which a current flows
- how many safety features use Lenz's law

**Competences:**
- understanding a text about generators
- understanding a technical diagram
- understanding spoken instructions
- using a diagram to explain a principle

## 1 Generators

★ a) Study the diagram and the text and find the English equivalents of the German words.

An electric generator has a wire (conductor), wound in loops (armature) which is rotated through the magnetic field of a magnet. Each time the wire moves across the magnetic field, the free electrons move to one end of the wire and produce a voltage (tension). The direction of the movement of electrons changes with the direction of the movement of the wire. In the diagram the circular movement of the armature generates an alternating current (AC). If the ends of the wire are joined together, there is a flow of electrons, and this generates a current which can power a load. The current in the moving wire produces its own magnetic field which combines with the magnetic field of the magnet and opposes the movement of the wire (see Lenz's Law, p. 13).

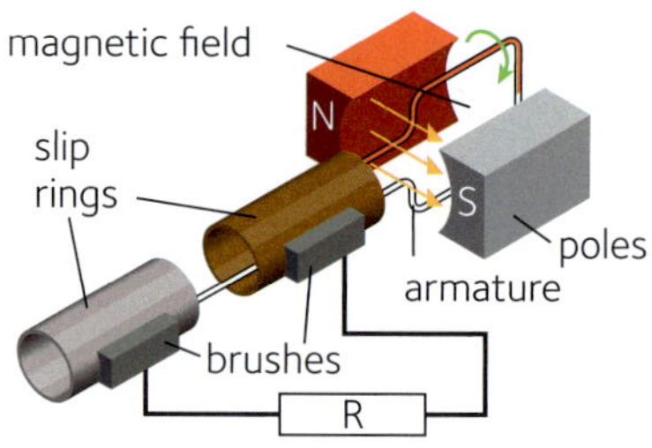


1 Bürste ______________________
2 Draht ______________________
3 Wicklung ______________________
4 Spannung ______________________
5 Richtung ______________________
6 zusammenfügen ______________________
7 Last ______________________
8 sich widersetzen ______________________

★★ b) Use the text and the diagram above to complete the sentences below.

1 An armature is ______________________.
2 A voltage is only produced when the wire moves ______________________.
3 If the wire moves in a different direction, the electrons ______________________.
4 In the generator shown, alternating current is generated because ______________________.
5 A load can be powered if ______________________.
6 A second magnetic field is produced by ______________________.

★★★ c) Use the information in the text above and the diagram to complete the sentences.

| 1 | Current flows through the conductor when you move it |
|---|---|
| a | in the direction of the magnetic field (left and right). |
| b | across the magnetic field (up and down). |
| c | in any direction in the magnetic field. |

| 2 | The current flows |
|---|---|
| a | in different directions depending on which way the conductor is moved. |
| b | in the same direction no matter which way the conductor is moved. |
| c | only when the conductor is moved downwards. |

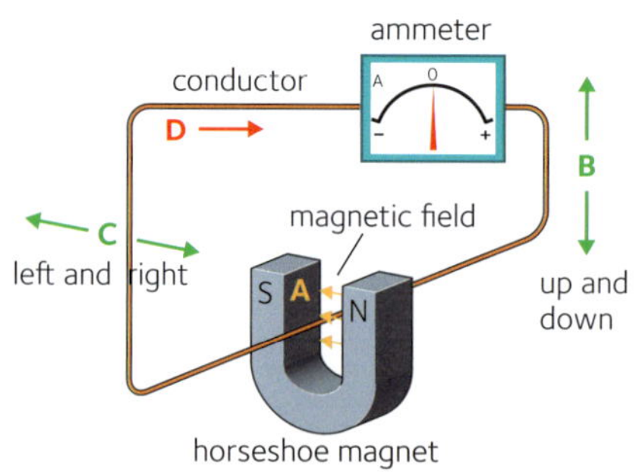


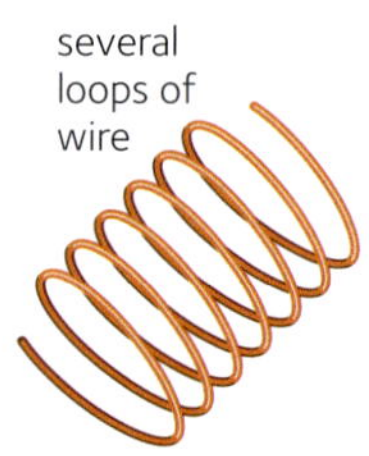


| 3 | The current is greatest when the conductor |
|---|---|
| a | is moved slowly. |
| b | isn't moved. |
| c | is moved fast. |

| 4 | If a stronger magnet is used, |
|---|---|
| a | the current is weaker. |
| b | the current is stronger. |
| c | it makes no difference. |

## 2 Fleming's right-hand rule

It is helpful for an electrician to know Fleming's right-hand rule. Use the diagram to complete the explanation below.

Fleming's right-hand rule

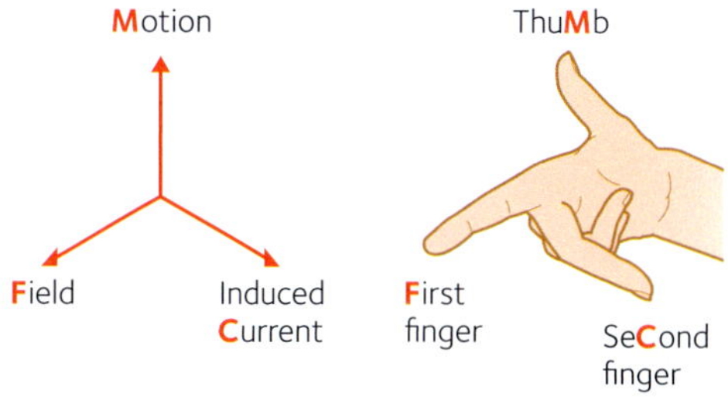


When a conductor is moved across a magnetic field, a voltage is induced (generated) in the conductor. The direction in which the ________________[1] flows in an electric circuit depends on the polarity of the magnetic ________________[2] and the direction of the ________________[3].

5

## 3 Lenz's Law

Safety features based on Lenz's Law can be found in a wide variety of appliances, including electric car and train brakes, safety brakes on lifts and free-fall towers in amusement parks.

★ a) Study the following explanation and the tip box, then complete the sentences in the table.

The strength of the voltage depends on
- the speed at which the conductor moves across the field (or the magnetic field moves past the conductor).
- the strength of the magnetic field.
- the number of loops in the conductor.

**Lenz's Law**

The magnetic field induced in a conductor opposes the cause.

<table>
<tr><td>1</td><td>The weaker the magnetic field,</td><td rowspan="6">the stronger<br>the weaker</td><td rowspan="6">the current.</td></tr>
<tr><td>2</td><td>The fewer loops the conductor has,</td></tr>
<tr><td>3</td><td>The stronger the magnetic field,</td></tr>
<tr><td>4</td><td>The faster the conductor moves,</td></tr>
<tr><td>5</td><td>The slower the conductor moves,</td></tr>
<tr><td>6</td><td>The more loops the conductor has,</td></tr>
</table>

★★ b) Listen to the description of an experiment with Lenz's Law and fill in the gaps in the text.

For this experiment we need a permanent magnet and a coil, which is a ________________[1] made up of many turns of ________________[2] wire. The two ends of the coil are not joined together. First we hold the coil over the magnet and ________________[3] it between the poles. It falls quickly at the speed of ________________[4]. Next, we join the ends of the wire together and drop the coil between the poles again. This time it falls slowly and ________________[5]. Why does it fall like this the second time? It does so because the ________________[6] of the coil induced a ________________[7] in it. This produced a second magnetic field which acted ________________[8] the movement of the coil and slowed its fall.

★★★ c) Draw and label a diagram (or diagrams) of the above experiment.

**IT'S YOUR TURN**

Find an application on the Internet that uses Lenz's law and make a poster with pictures and texts to explain how it works.

# Extra practice: Units 1–4

## 1 The German apprenticeship system

You have English-speaking visitors at your college and they ask you to explain how electricians are trained in Germany, so you draw a diagram to show how your apprenticeship is organized.
Fill in the gaps in the diagram using the information in unit 1.

APPRENTICE ELECTRICIANS' TRAINING COURSE

| | TIME | CONTENT |
|---|---|---|
| BASIC TRAINING | ______ year | |
| SPECIALIST TRAINING | ______ years | Either: ______<br>Or: ______<br>Or: ______<br>Or: ______ |

## 2 The basic principles of electricity

A friend asks you to correct his English essay on the basic principles of electricity. You check it and find ten factual mistakes. Underline the mistakes and correct them.

The atom is made up of protons, electrons and neutrons, and if the neutrons are separated from the protons they try to flow back to them. This flow of atomic particles is called the voltage. A material through which electricity can flow easily is called a resistance, e.g. plastic. The mathematical relationship between current, voltage and resistance is shown by the equation V= I × R, whereby V stands for current, I stands for resistance and R stands for voltage. Resistance is measured in volts. The most common source of alternating current is a wet cell battery.

## 3 Explaining how an electrical device works

You have to give a presentation at college in English to explain how an electric torch (*AE*: flashlight) works.

a) Label points 1–7 on the diagram and add further information of your own, e.g. the polarity of the batteries, the direction of the electron flow, the material the spring is made of, etc.

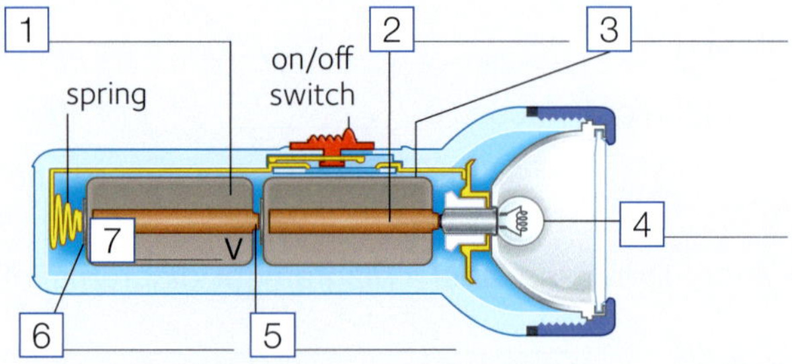


b) Practise giving the presentation to a partner, then give it to the whole class.

## 4 Hydroelectric power generation

Hydroelectricity is the most widely used form of renewable energy. As an electrician you need to know how a hydroelectric generator works. Look at the text in unit 4 (Generators), then write a short text explaining how water power is used to generate electricity at a hydroelectric power station. Explain how the generator works and why the current produced is AC. Use the language box.

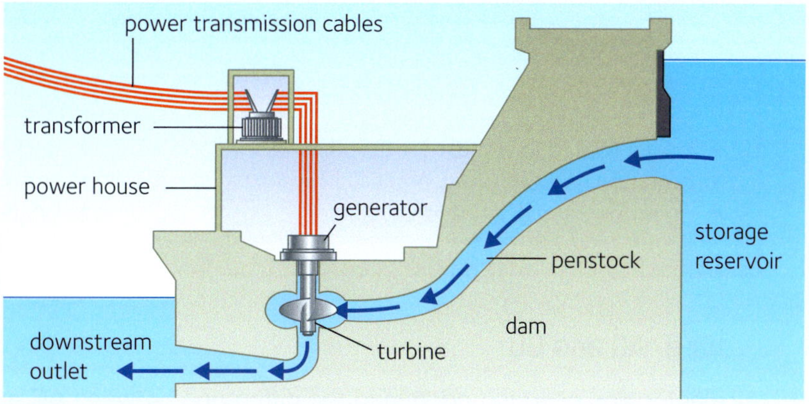


| | | | | | |
|---|---|---|---|---|---|
| to flow | to turn | to generate | to transmit | a coil | a magnet |

## ▶▶▶ ICH KANN

| | | Seite/Übung |
|---|---|---|
| ☐ | Ich kann in einfachen zusammenhängenden Sätzen Diagramme beschreiben und interpretieren. B1 | 9/ It's your turn |
| ☐ | Ich kann berufs- oder fachbezogene Sachverhalte und Prozesse (z. B. Elektrizität) einfach, aber strukturiert beschreiben, erklären bzw. zusammenfassen. B1 | 7/ It's your turn |
| ☐ | Ich kann an einfachen Gesprächen teilnehmen (z. B. Ausbildung). Ich kann dabei auch zeigen, dass ich mich für das interessiere, was mir jemand sagt. A2 | 4/1b |
| ☐ | Ich kann kurzen und deutlich gesprochenen Texten und Tonträgern die wesentlichen Informationen entnehmen, wenn es um vorhersehbare alltägliche oder berufsspezifisch vertraute Dinge (z. B. Beschreibung von Elektrizität, Gleichstrom, *Lenz's Law*) geht. A2 | 6/1a; 9/3; 11/3b |
| ☐ | Ich kann Interviews, Berichten und Vorträgen in den wesentlichen Punkten folgen. B1 | 4/1a |
| ☐ | Ich kann einfachen Alltagstexten, die sich auf vertraute Situationen beziehen, die wichtigsten Informationen entnehmen (z. B. berufliche Alltagsbeschreibungen). A2 | 5/2b; 7/2b |
| ☐ | Ich kann einfache Sachtexte (z. B. Beschreibung von Strom und Stromspannung) verstehen, wenn Bilder oder Grafiken den Inhalt unterstützen. A2 | 7/1a; 10/1a,b,c; 11/2 |
| ☐ | Ich kann Sachtexte verstehen, die einfach und für ein breites Publikum geschrieben sind und in denen es um Themen geht, die mit meinen Interessen oder meinem Fachgebiet in Zusammenhang stehen. B1 | 11/3a |
| ☐ | Ich kann Informationen in verschiedenen längeren Texten oder Textteilen finden, die ich brauche, um eine bestimmte Aufgabe zu lösen. B1 | 6/1b,c; 8/1a,b,c |
| ☐ | Ich kann aus vorgegebenen Wörtern einfache Sätze bilden und aufschreiben. A1 | 9/4 |
| ☐ | Ich kann einen kurzen, einfachen Text über ein persönliches Erlebnis oder eine Erfahrung (z. B. in der Ausbildung) schreiben. A2 | 4/1c |

# 5 DC and AC

**This unit is about:**
- how a light bulb works
- common sources of AC and DC power
- common uses of AC and DC power

**Competences:**
- understanding a technical text
- selecting a suitable power source
- listening to a recording
- explaining how an electrical device works

## 1 AC and DC

All electricians need to understand the difference between AC and DC current.

★ a) Study the text below and find the English equivalents of the German words.

1 je nach ____________________
2 hin und her ____________________
3 dünn ____________________
4 sich reiben ____________________
5 Reibung ____________________
6 glühen ____________________
7 Leiter ____________________
8 Wissenschaftler/in ____________________
9 entgegen ____________________
10 geladen ____________________

★★ b) Read the text and say which type of current is in each copper conductor. Then label the three parts of the traditional light bulb and say if the power source is AC or DC.

When you connect a power source to an electric circuit such as a length of copper wire, the current which flows is either direct current (DC) or alternating current (AC), depending on the source. With DC the electrons in the conductor all travel in the same direction. With AC they just move to and fro. Both DC and AC can power a load, e.g. a light bulb.
When the electrons move in the thin filament of a light bulb, they rub against each other and other atoms and the friction they produce heats up the filament and makes it glow. It makes no difference whether the electrons travel along the conductor or just move to and fro. It's only important that they move.
Before scientists knew about the structure of the atom and the movement of electrons, they believed that electric current flowed from the positive to the negative terminal. Today we know that negatively-charged electrons flow towards the protons, which are positive. (See unit 2 What is electricity?) However, current is still defined as a flow of electrically charged particles from the positive to the negative terminal of a voltage source.

copper conductor 1: __________

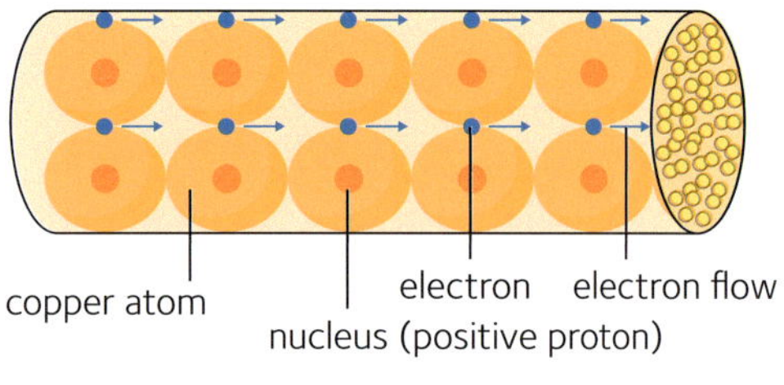


copper conductor 2: __________

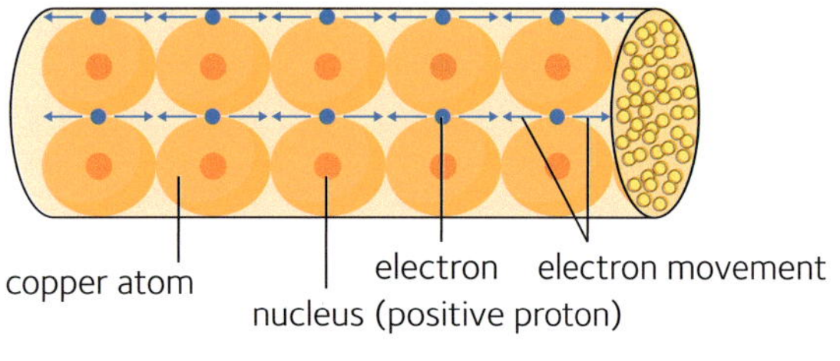


light bulb

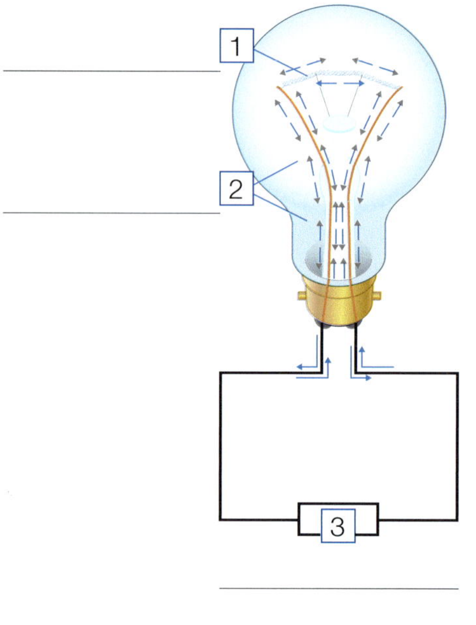

★★★ c) Fill in the gaps with words from the text.

If the ______________[1] in a closed electrical ______________[2] flows in one direction only, it is called ______________[3] current. If the electrons move to and ______________[4], it is called ______________[5] current. In the closed circuit the electrons in the thin ______________[6] of a light bulb ______________[7] against each other and the light bulb shines brightly. This is because the ______________[8] between the electrons ______________[9] up the filament and makes it ______________[10].

## 2 Electrical devices

Neon lights and many bigger electric motors use AC, but most electronic devices such as hi-fi and video equipment use DC from (rechargeable) batteries or from an external AC source such as the mains. In this case the AC mains voltage of 230V is first transformed to an acceptable level (e.g. 3 volts) and then rectified to DC.

★ a) Label the devices below with the words in the box.

cordless drill • electric motor • mouse • power drill

1 
Shutterstock/Theerawut_SS

______________

2 
Fotolia.com/naruedom

______________

3 
Shutterstock/AG-Photos

______________

4 
Shutterstock/yevgeniy11

______________

★★ b) Name the power source for each device.

1 ______________ 2 ______________ 3 ______________ 4 ______________

★★★ c) Say if the power source is AC or DC for each device.

1 ______________ 2 ______________ 3 ______________ 4 ______________

## 6 3 Parts of the drill

Listen to the recording about an electric drill and use the words in the box to label the parts of the drill.

armature • brushes • commutator • electronic speed control unit • gearwheel • mains lead • push button switch • stator

1 ______________________
2 ______________________
3 ______________________
4 ______________________
5 ______________________
6 ______________________
7 ______________________
8 ______________________

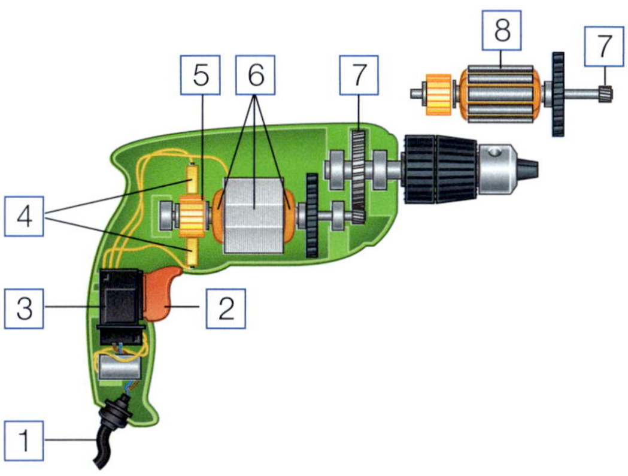


**IT'S YOUR TURN**

With a partner, prepare a short presentation of how another power tool works (e.g. an angle grinder, a belt sander, an electric saw) and give it to the class.

# 6 Electric circuits

**This unit is about:**
- common electrical components
- electrical circuits (schematics)
- units of resistance (ohm) and capacitance (farad)

**Competences:**
- understanding component symbols
- explaining how a component functions
- understanding a circuit diagram
- describing a circuit diagram

## 1 An electric circuit

Here are some typical symbols used electrical circuits.

antenna • capacitor • coil • crystal earpiece • diode • ground (earth) connection • LED • resistor • switch • variable capacitor

★ a) Name the symbols.

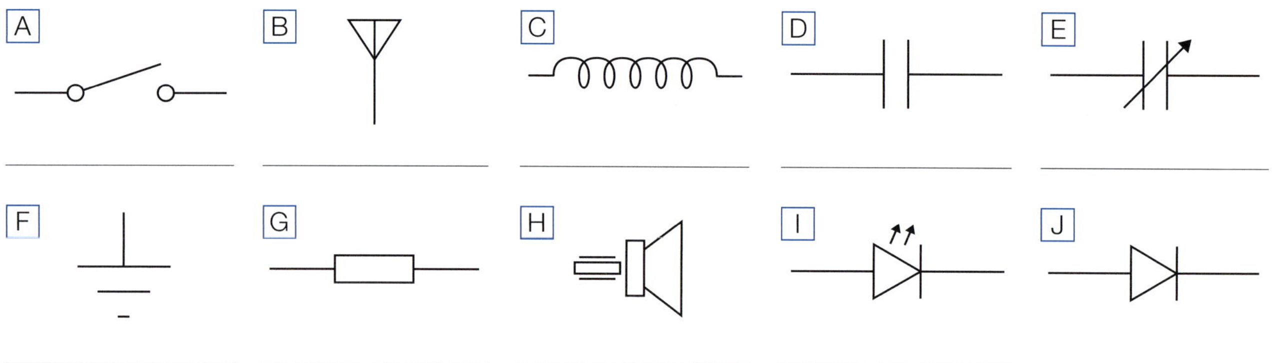


★★ b) Say which three of the following statements are false.

| | | T | F |
|---|---|---|---|
| 1 | A capacitor produces a magnetic field. | | |
| 2 | A coil produces light. | | |
| 3 | A resistor lowers the voltage. | | |
| 4 | An antenna changes electrical signals into sound. | | |
| 5 | A diode rectifies the current. | | |

★★★ c) Use the table below to correct the three false statements above. Then write a sentence about five other components.

| | | |
|---|---|---|
| | breaks | to earth. |
| | changes | light. |
| | leads | the circuit. |
| | lowers | a magnetic field. |
| A(n) … (component) | produces | the voltage. |
| | receives or transmits | the electrical charge stored. |
| | rectifies | an electric charge. |
| | stores | electrical signals into sounds. |
| | | the current. |

Corrected statements:

1 ______________________

2 ______________________

3 ______________________

Five other components:

1 ______________________

2 ______________________

3 ______________________

4 ______________________

5 ______________________

## 2 A circuit diagram

Work with a partner. Ask and answer questions about circuit diagram 1.

Example: *What's the component in square J4 called and what does it do? – It's a … and it …*

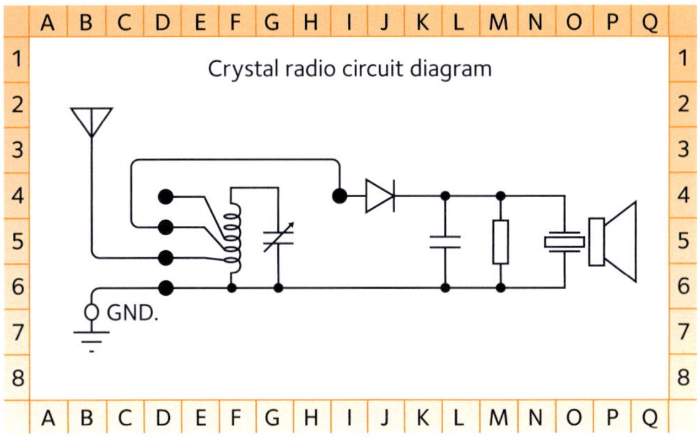


Circuit 1

## 3 Writing descriptions

Use this example and the language box to write descriptions of circuits 1 and 2.

This circuit consists of four resistors connected to a battery with a switch to turn the circuit on and off. Resistors $R_1$ and $R_2$ are alongside each other, so they are in parallel. Resistors $R_3$ and $R_4$ are after each other, so they are in series. Currents $I_1$ and $I_2$ are different from current $I_{Total}$. Voltage $V_1$ is different from $V_2$. There is an ammeter in the circuit between the switch and the resistors and the two voltmeters show the voltages across $R_3$ and $R_4$.

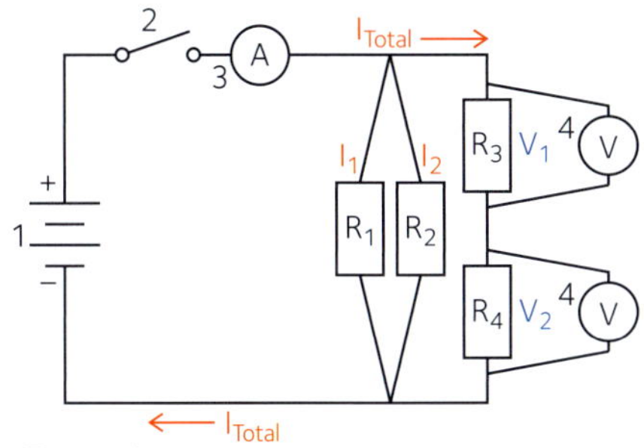


Example

| | |
|---|---|
| Circuit 1<br>Circuit 2 | consists of … |
| | is connected to …<br>is attached to … |
| | travels through / passes through … |
| | across/between/alongside is powered by |
| | is higher/lower than |
| | stays the same |
| | changes the … into … electrical signals sounds |

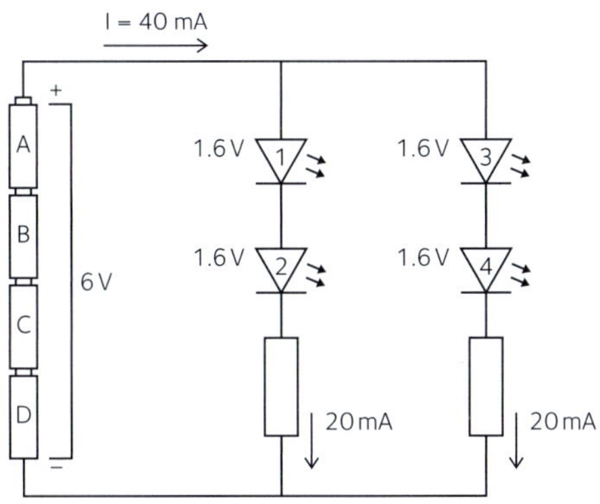


Circuit 2

7

## 4 Components in a circuit diagram

A teacher is talking to some students. Listen and label the components in the circuit diagram below. The tip box will help you.

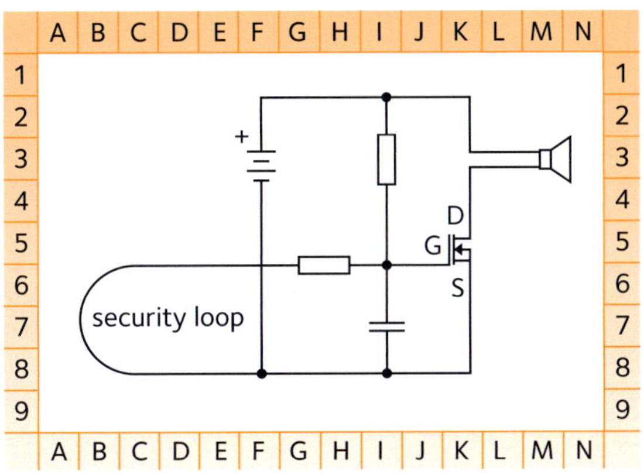


A simple alarm

| Tip | |
|---|---|
| We write | We say |
| Ω | ohm |
| 0 | zero |
| 1.5 | one point five |
| 1.55 | one point five five |
| 10 K | ten K |
| μF | microfarad |
| An example of a component number: BUK456 | B – U – K four five six |

**IT'S YOUR TURN**

As an electrician you need to be able to understand and describe a schematic. With a partner, write a description of the schematic in unit 18 exercise 1, Electronic control of currents, or of a schematic of your choice.

# 7 Electric power

**This unit is about:**

- joules, watts and kilowatt hours
- the relationships between voltage, current, resistance, energy and power

**Competences:**

- using mathematical symbols
- explaining an electrical problem
- solving an electrical problem

## 1 Electric power

What is a watt? Complete the sentences below with words from the text.

Energy is the same as work and is measured in joules. Power is work divided by time and is measured in watts. A joule is about how much energy is needed to lift a small apple (102 g) one metre. A watt is one joule of work per second. Therefore, if you lift an apple one metre in one second, you've done one watt of power.
A power station measures the electricity it supplies to a consumer in kilowatt hours (kWh). One kilowatt is one thousand watts and one hour is 3,600 seconds. One kilowatt hour is therefore 3,600,000 watt-seconds of work and costs about 30 cents. It would therefore only cost 30 cents to lift 3.6 million apples one metre. Would you do this for 30 cents?

1 A joule is a measure of ______________.
2 A watt is a measure of ______________.
3 Electricity consumption is measured in ______________.
4 A kilowatt is ______________________.

## 2 Power consumption

Here are some typical, everyday electrical appliances.

★★ a) Match the appliances with their normal wattages.

| | | | |
|---|---|---|---|
| 1 | CD player | a | 1,600 W |
| 2 | hairdryer | b | 2,400 W |
| 3 | electric drill | c | 14 W |
| 4 | tumble dryer | d | 450 W |

★★★ b) Complete the following sentences with two words from the box.

less/least • more/most • powerful • power

1 A hairdryer uses ______________ than a CD player.
2 Of all the appliances here, the tumble dryer uses the ______________.
3 A CD player is ______________ than an electric drill.
4 The CD player is the ______________ of all the four appliances.
5 An electric drill is ______________ than a CD player but ______________ than a tumble dryer.

**Tip**

**Mathematical signs**

| | |
|---|---|
| = | equals |
| + | plus |
| – | minus |
| × | times |
| ÷ | divided by |
| ≈ 4 | about/approximately equal to |
| $4^2$ | four squared |
| √16 | the square root of |
| 1.462 | one point four six two |

**Language tips**

- For the equation $5 = \frac{10}{2}$ you can say:
  Five equals ten divided by two, or
  Five equals ten over two.
- In English, long numbers are separated by commas: 2,840,782.
- a 60 W bulb = a sixty-watt bulb ("watt" is an adjective: → no plural)
  The bulb was 60 watts. ("watt" is a noun: → plural)

## 3 Ohm's Law

What do you know about Ohm's Law?

★ a) Match each sentence (1–6) with an Ohm's Law equation (1–12).

| Ohm's Law equations | | | | | | | |
|---|---|---|---|---|---|---|---|
| Current (I) | ① $\frac{E}{R}$ | ② $\frac{P}{E}$ | ③ $\frac{\sqrt{P}}{R}$ | Resistance (R) | ④ $\frac{E}{I}$ | ⑤ $\frac{E^2}{P}$ | ⑥ $\frac{P}{I^2}$ |
| Voltage (E) | ⑦ $I \times R$ | ⑧ $\frac{P}{I}$ | ⑨ $\sqrt{P \times R}$ | Power (P) | ⑩ $E \times I$ | ⑪ $I^2 \times R$ | ⑫ $\frac{E^2}{R}$ |

1 Voltage equals current times resistance. ☐
2 Power equals current squared times resistance. ☐
3 Voltage equals the square root of power times resistance. ☐
4 Resistance equals voltage squared over power. ☐
5 Power equals voltage squared divided by resistance. ☐
6 Current equals voltage over resistance. ☐

**Tip**

In German U stands for voltage.
In English it can be E or V.

★★ b) Complete the equations below with expressions from the exercise above and say which equation they are (1–12).

1 Power equals voltage ______________ current. Equation no. ________
2 Resistance equals voltage ______________ current. Equation no. ________
3 Current equals ____________________ power over resistance. Equation no. ________
4 Voltage equals power ______________ current. Equation no. ________

★★★ c) Which two equations have not yet been defined in exercises a) and b)? Find them and write them out in full.

______________________________________________________________

______________________________________________________________

8 🎧

## 4 Writing summaries

Two customers phone with problems. Listen and make notes. Then write very short summaries in your exercise book and work out the values using a suitable Ohm's Law equation.

1 A customer in an electronics shop has a problem: ______________________________

______________________________________________ Equation: ______________

Emily Jones is calling an electrical contractor: ______________________________

______________________________________________________________

______________________________________________ Equation: ______________

**IT'S YOUR TURN**

A customer phones your company with the following problem:
"I have a washing machine and a tumble dryer. A workman came to do some work in the house and unplugged the dryer to plug in his extension reel. I needed to use both the dryer and the washing machine at the same time, so I plugged them into the same socket with an adapter. When I switched on the washing machine, everything was fine but when I switched on the dryer, all the lights went out."
Role-play this situation with a partner. Explain what happened and offer suitable advice.

# 8 Power distribution

**This unit is about:**
- AC power distribution
- DC power distribution
- why blackouts happen

**Competences:**
- understanding a text about power distribution
- talking about blackouts
- applying Ohm's Law in an everyday situation

## 1 Power distribution

This text explains how power gets to our homes.

★ a) Study the text and find the English equivalents of the German words.

1 Kraftwerk ______________ 2 Wechselstrom ______________ 3 übertragen ______________
4 hochtransformiert ______________ 5 Transformator ______________ 6 Umspannwerk ______________
7 heruntertransformiert ______________ 8 Verbraucher/in ______________ 9 Gleichstrom ______________
10 geeignet ______________

★★ b) Label the diagrams with the words and numbers in blue from the text.

Power stations generate alternating current because it is easy to transmit over long distances. The electricity leaves the station at about 25,000 V and it is then stepped up to 380,000 V by transformers at electrical substations. It then travels overland through overhead high-tension cables on pylons until it reaches its destination. There it is stepped down to about 20,000 V at other substations and sent along overhead or underground cables to near where it is needed. Step-down transformers are then used to reduce the final voltage to 230 V or 400 V for the consumer. Nowadays, modern high-voltage direct current (HVDC) systems are becoming more and more popular for long-distance electricity transmission because they can transmit up to five times more power through existing power lines and are also better suited for underground or undersea cables.

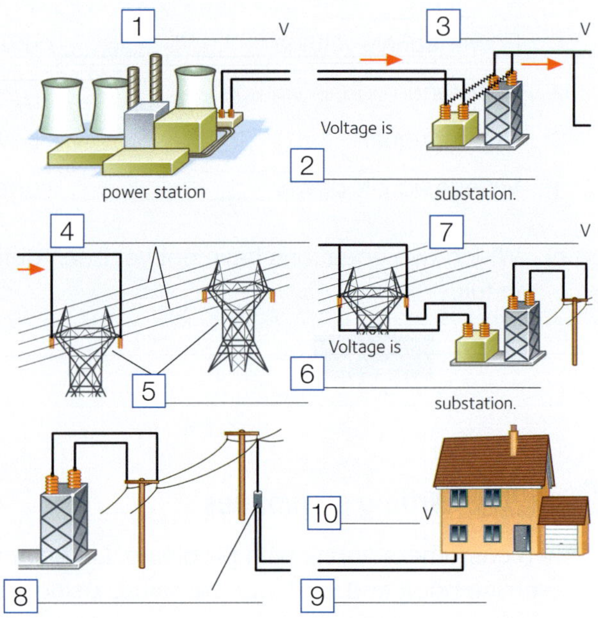


## 2 A blackout

Blackouts can affect large areas and last for days. The text below is about a blackout in New York City in 1977. Fill in the gaps with a simple past form from the box.

arrested • damaged • hit • made • overloaded • reduced • started • took • was • were

At 8.37 p.m. on July 13, 1977 lightning ____________ [1] a substation near New York City. A second strike eight minutes later badly ____________ [2] two 345 kV transmission lines. A third strike at 8.55 p.m. ____________ [3] two more lines fail and this ____________ [4] the whole grid. The power company then ____________ [5] the voltage by 8% but this ____________ [6] not enough. A chain reaction ____________ [7] and at 9.27 p.m., just 50 minutes after the first lightning strike, New Yorkers ____________ [8] without electricity. It ____________ [9] almost another 24 hours to get the power back and that night the police ____________ [10] 4,500 looters.

## 3 Would they work in a blackout?

Do you know what appliances would work in a blackout so you could advise customers?

★ a) Match the pictures with the words in the list.

1

Fotolia.com/Kaspars Grinvalds

______________

2

Fotolia.com/ftiero

______________

3

Shutterstock/Lupco Smokovski

______________

4

Fotolia.com/zhu difeng

______________

calculator • cooker • fridge • lamp • laptop computer • lift • mobile phone • TV

5

Fotolia.com/Tiramisu Studio

______________

6

Fotolia.com/Kurhan

______________

7

Fotolia.com/chagin

______________

8

Shutterstock/Li Chaoshu

______________

★★ b) Use the table to explain what would happen in a blackout. Write in your exercise book.

| | | | | |
|---|---|---|---|---|
| | | | runs | off the mains. |
| | | | doesn't run | a 230V power supply. |
| | | | needs | on batteries. |
| In a blackout, the … | would<br>wouldn't | work because it | doesn't need | its own power supply. |
| | | | has | rechargeable. |
| | | | doesn't have | electricity all the time. |
| | | | is/isn't | |

★★★ c) Explain why some of the devices pictured above would stop working instantly in a blackout but others would take longer.

9

## 4 An electricity supplier

An old lady has a problem. Listen to the dialogue between her and her electricity supplier and complete the sentences below. The words in the box will help you.

1 Doris wants to speak to a ______________ .
2 She thinks there has been ______________ .
3 Doris has never heard of ______________ .
4 Older people call it ______________ .
5 The lights went off when she was making ______________ .
6 When Doris used the metal knife she ______________ the toaster.
7 The technician first tells Doris ______________ the toaster.
8 Then he tells her to check the ______________ .
9 Finally, he tells her to push up the big switch in the main ______________ .
10 He advises her never to use a ______________ in a toaster.

- circuit-breaker
- circuit-breakers
- to disconnect
- some toast
- the consumer unit
- the fuse box
- a power cut
- short-circuited
- metal knife
- technician

**IT'S YOUR TURN**

Work with a partner and research on the Internet to give a short presentation to the class about one of the following topics: the war of the currents; HVAC vs HVDC or the increasing need for DC power.

# Extra practice: Units 5–8

## 1 How light bulbs work

This text explains how a light bulb works.

★ a) Read the text and label the diagram of a CFL, a compact fluorescent lamp (1–8).

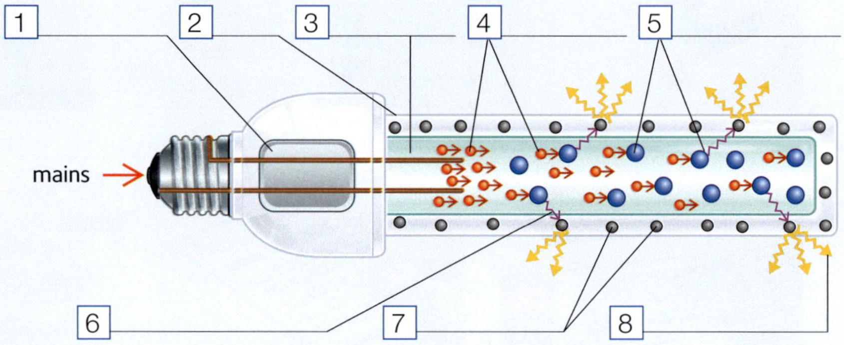


When the lamp is plugged in, electricity flows from the mains to a transformer in the base of the lamp and the voltage is increased. It then flows to two electrodes which are in a tube filled with mercury gas, here shown as light blue circles. The electrodes release electrons (red) which collide with the mercury atoms. These collisions produce photons of invisible ultraviolet light (violet zigzags in the diagram). The inner tube of the lamp is coated with phosphors (grey circles) and when the ultraviolet light hits them, they give off photons of visible white light.

★★ b) Use your own knowledge, your textbook or research on the Internet to label the diagram of a halogen light bulb. Add any extra information you think is important.

★★★ c) Work with a partner and write a text describing how a halogen light bulb works.

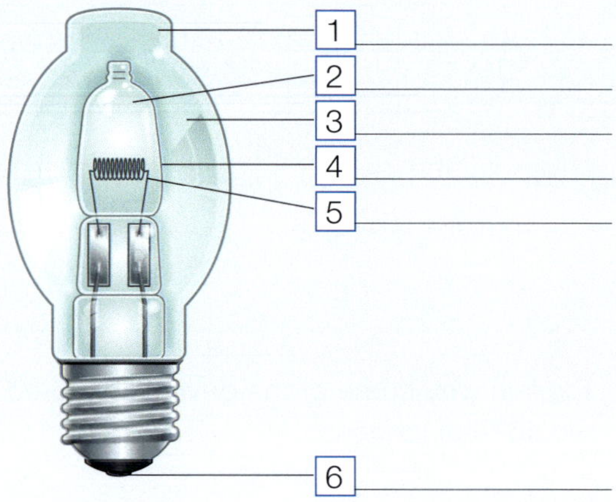


## 2 Electrical components

Name as many components as you can in the circuit diagram below of a battery charger (LM117T is a voltage regulator). Use your electrical engineering textbook and/or the Internet for any extra information needed.

Make your list like this: *G 6 – voltage regulator, B 6 – fuse …*

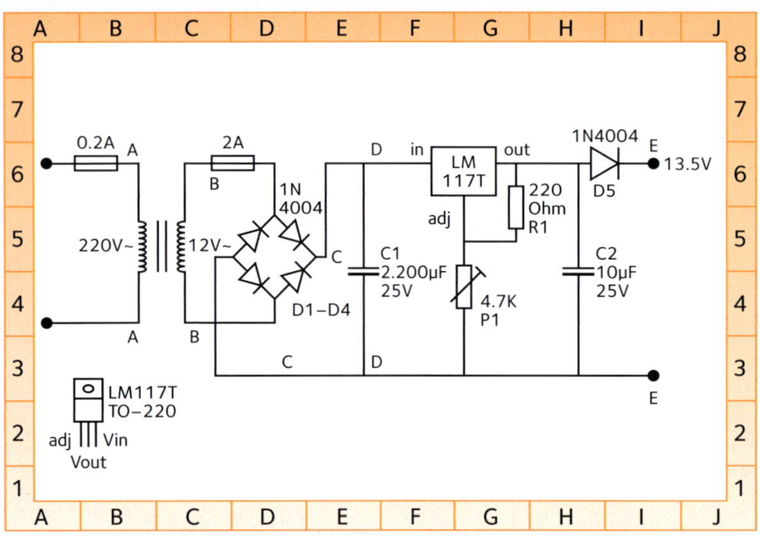

## 3 The power supplies of the future

A BBC reporter for Technology Today is asking the managing director of a major German electricity company how electricity will be transmitted over long distances in the future.
Work with a partner and take it in turns to play the two roles.

| John Kelly, BBC reporter | Julia Beck, Managing Director |
|---|---|
| Today our studio guest is Julia Beck. She's the MD of a big German electricity company. Welcome to the show! | Bedanken Sie sich für die Einladung. |
| We've heard so much about electricity from offshore wind turbines or solar power from the hot regions of the earth, but is it realistic to transmit electricity so far to a country like Germany? | Sie stimmen zu, dass die Wege sehr lang sind, aber es gibt eine Alternative zur konventionellen Drehstrom-Hochspannungs-Übertragung (engl. HVAC) mit Umspannwerken. |
| Now you've got me interested! Do you perhaps mean rechargeable batteries in every household? | Erklären Sie, dass einige amerikanische Firmen bereits an solchen Systemen arbeiten. Sie meinen aber die Hochspannungs-Gleichstrom-Übertragung (engl. HVDC). |
| That sounds complicated! Can you give our listeners some more details? | Erläutern Sie die Eigenschaften und Vorteile der HGÜ. |
| Thanks for telling us what the future will bring! | Bedanken Sie sich für die Möglichkeit, über die Zukunft des Stromnetzes zu sprechen. |

## ▶▶▶ ICH KANN

| | Seite/Übung |
|---|---|
| ☐ Ich kann berufs- oder fachbezogene Sachverhalte und Prozesse (z. B. Elektrizität) einfach, aber strukturiert beschreiben, erklären bzw. zusammenfassen. B1 | 15/ It's your turn |
| ☐ Ich kann an einfachen Gesprächen teilnehmen (z. B. Ausbildung). Ich kann dabei auch zeigen, dass ich mich für das interessiere, was mir jemand sagt. A2 | 17/2 |
| ☐ Ich kann eine Rolle in einem Dialog oder einer Simulation übernehmen (z. B. Berufssituation). A2 | 19/ It's your turn |
| ☐ Ich kann kurzen und deutlich gesprochenen Texten und Tonträgern die wesentlichen Informationen entnehmen, wenn es um vorhersehbare alltägliche oder berufsspezifisch vertraute Dinge (z. B. Beschreibung von Elektrizität, Gleichstrom, *Lenz's Law*) geht. A2 | 15/3; 17/4; 19/4; 21/4 |
| ☐ Ich kann einfachen Alltagstexten, die sich auf vertraute Situationen beziehen, die wichtigsten Informationen entnehmen (z. B. berufliche Alltagsbeschreibungen, Gleich-/Wechselstrom). A2 | 14/1a |
| ☐ Ich kann einfache Sachtexte (z. B. Beschreibung von Strom und Stromspannung) verstehen, wenn Bilder oder Grafiken den Inhalt unterstützen. A2 | 14/1b; 19/3a, b, c |
| ☐ Ich kann Informationen in verschiedenen längeren Texten oder Textteilen finden, die ich brauche, um eine bestimmte Aufgabe zu lösen. B1 | 14/1c; 16/1b; 18/1; 20/1a,b |
| ☐ Ich kann Wörter und Sätze richtig abschreiben. A1 | 15/2a; 16/1a; 18/2a, b; 21/3a, b |
| ☐ Ich kann aus vorgegebenen Wörtern einfache Sätze bilden und aufschreiben. A1 | 16/1c; 17/3 |

# 9 Storing electrical energy

**This unit is about:**
- storing electrical energy
- capacitors
- how to reduce energy costs

**Competences:**
- reading about capacitors
- understanding a technical diagram
- explaining how efficient a device is

## 1 Storing electrical energy

There are different ways of storing electrical energy.

★ a) Complete the sentences below with words from the text.

Fotolia.com/Andrej Kaprinay

If you only need a small amount of electrical energy over a period of time for a device such as a torch or a mobile phone, a rechargeable or non-rechargeable battery is enough. However, if you need a small amount of power very quickly, you need a capacitor. Capacitors don't generate electricity with a chemical reaction like a battery. They only store electrons and can release them in a fraction of a second, which means that they can also be very dangerous. A camera flash unit, for example, has a capacitor. Capacitors can also be recharged in a few seconds and used over and over again, and nowadays so-called supercapacitors even power electric buses. They run without overhead power lines and are quickly recharged each time they stop. Storing power for the power grid is a very different problem because of the huge quantities of energy needed. One answer is a pumped storage power plant using water (e.g. Goldisthal in Thuringia) which can store thousands of kilowatts of off-peak electricity for later use. Another solution is a compressed air energy storage plant such as the Iowa Stored Energy Park in the USA.

1 A mobile phone uses a ______________________.
2 Capacitors deliver power ______________.
3 A capacitor doesn't ______________________.
4 Capacitors can be dangerous because ______________________________________________.
5 You can recharge a capacitor in __________.
6 Buses with supercapacitors don't need ______________________.
7 Huge quantities of energy are needed for ______________________.
8 Large quantities of power can be stored at ______________________________________________.

★★ b) Label the pictures of devices using capacitors and then translate them into German.

fork-lift truck • MRI scanner • plasma TV • X-ray machine

Fotolia.com/Space-kraft

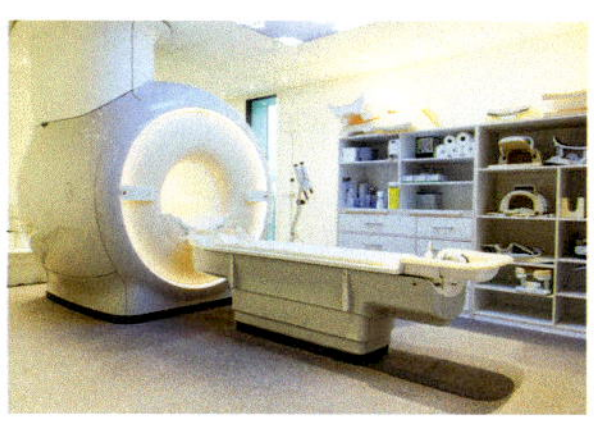
Fotolia.com/digitalefotografien

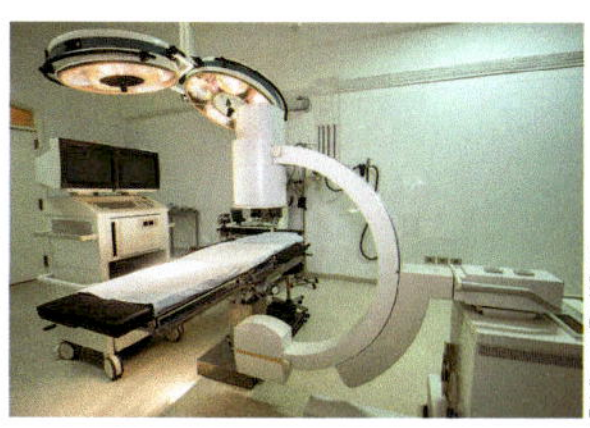
Fotolia.com/Paul Vinten

Shutterstock/Semisatch

______________ ______________ ______________ ______________

______________ ______________ ______________ ______________

★★★ c) Can you think of other devices powered by capacitors? Make a list in your exercise book.

## 2 A pumped storage power plant

Today, storing energy is an important issue. Use words from the diagram to fill in the gaps in the text.

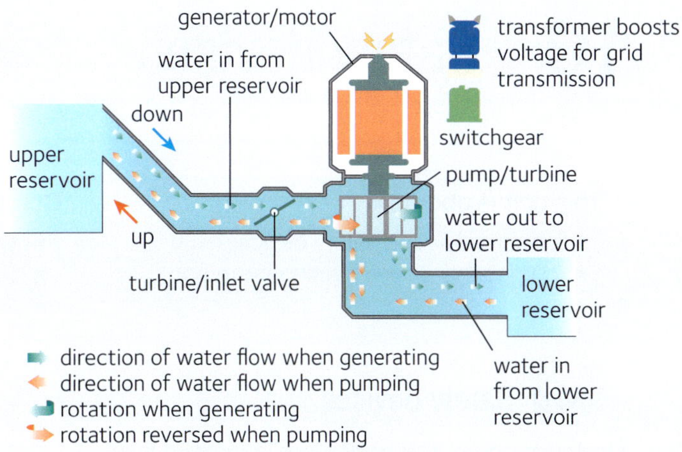


Pumped storage power plant

A pumped ____________[1] power plant is one of the most efficient ways of storing a very large quantity of power. Water is pumped from a lower to an upper ____________[2] with an electric ____________[3] which drives a ____________[4] at times when there is extra power. On its way ____________[5] the water passes through an ____________[6] and is stored until needed. Later, when more electricity is needed it flows ____________[7] to the lower level and spins a ____________[8] which generates electricity. The electricity generated first goes through a ____________[9] unit and is then stepped up to a much higher ____________[10] by a ____________[11] before it enters the power ____________[12].

## 3 Energy plant

When is it cool to buy a new fridge? Study the table and the US government's EnergyGuide label on all new fridges and then fill in the gaps.

| If your fridge was made before/ between/after | it uses about this much energy per year. | Replacing it with an energy-efficient model will save about |
|---|---|---|
| <1976 | 1800 kWh | $151 per year |
| 1976–86 | 1400 kWh | $107 per year |
| 1987–89 | 950 kWh | $58 per year |
| 1990–92 | 900 kWh | $52 per year |
| 1993–00 | 700 kWh | $30 per year |
| 2001+ | 500 kWh | $8 per year |

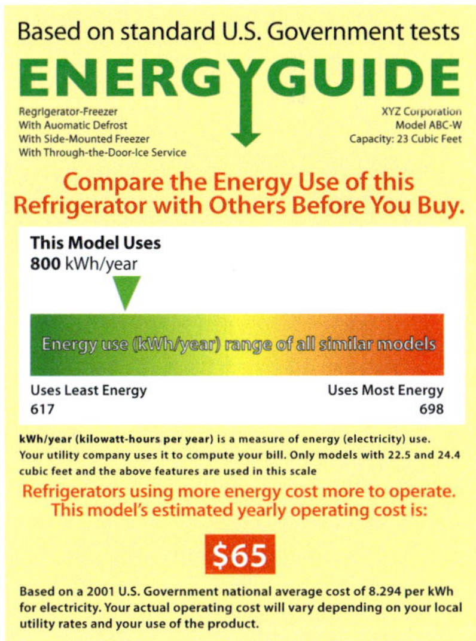


Large fridges made ____________[1] 1976 use about ____________[2] of electricity per year. If you replace a very old fridge with a new ____________[3] model you can save about ____________[4] per year. The EnergyGuide label here shows that the fridge in question uses ____________[5] of electricity and costs ____________[6] to operate per year. The table shows that a fridge made between ____________[7] and ____________[8] only uses half as much electricity as one made before 1976. If your fridge was made after ____________[9] it will use only about 500 ____________[10] of electricity per year so you'll only save about ____________[11] per year if you buy a new one.

**IT'S YOUR TURN**

A customer wants to know the cost of running her electrical appliances.
Work with a partner and look at the specification plates on your fridge / electric cooker / dishwasher / washing machine / computer / stereo or other device and work out how much power it costs to operate them at maximum performance for 1 hour. Next work out how much they cost to run for a year. Find out the price of 1 kWh from your energy supplier or assume it's 0.1535 €/kWh. Use a watt-hour meter (power measuring meter) if you have one. Present your results to the class.

# 10 Safety devices

**This unit is about:**
- commonly used safety devices
- comparing different wiring systems

**Competences:**
- understanding technical descriptions
- understanding a diagram about household wiring systems
- listening to a recording

## 1 Safety devices

Understanding safety devices can save lives.

★ a) Study the text and find the English equivalents of the German words.

1 Stromkreis ____________ 2 Sicherheitsvorrichtung ____________ 3 überlasten ____________
4 beschädigen ____________ 5 verletzen ____________ 6 durchbrennen ____________
7 ersetzen ____________ 8 sich auslösen ____________ 9 schützen ____________
10 Fehlstrom ____________

Electrical engineers make sure a circuit has a weak point which breaks first if it is overloaded. This stops the circuit from overheating, catching fire, damaging equipment and harming people.

There are three types of safety devices in electrical circuits:
A fuse – it blows. This means it breaks when overloaded. You can't reset it, so you replace the whole fuse, e.g. a blade fuse in a car or a cartridge fuse in an electrical device or the wire in a rewirable fuse (only used in the UK) because it burns through. Fuses are cheap.
A circuit breaker – It trips when overloaded and can be reset. It protects electrical appliances, e.g. a toaster or a washing machine but doesn't protect people because it lets a lot of current through, e.g. 16 A, before it trips. Circuit breakers are expensive.
An RCD (residual current device) – It trips when overloaded and can be reset. It is highly sensitive and trips if there's a fault current of as little as 30 mA. Its job is to protect people and it is used in bathrooms and for outside devices, e.g. the socket for a hedge trimmer. RCDs are expensive.

★★ b) Use words from the text to name the five safety devices and write their German equivalents.

1

____________
____________

2

____________
____________

3
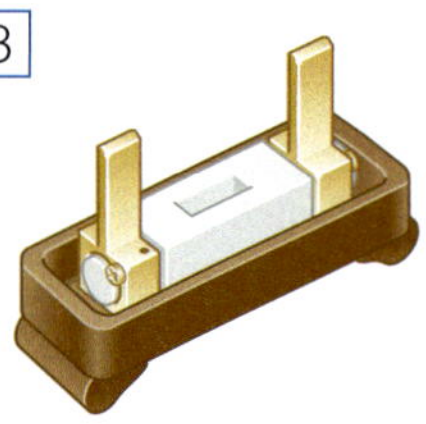
____________
____________

4
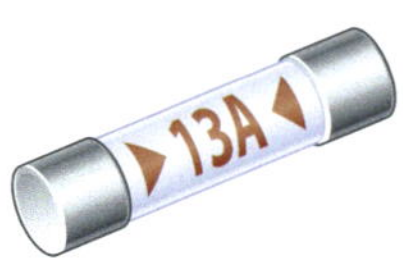

____________
____________

5

____________
____________

★★★ c) Match the sentence halves.

1 A fuse is the part of the circuit
2 A fuse can't
3 When a fuse is overloaded,
4 Circuit breakers
5 A circuit breaker costs
6 When a circuit breaker is overloaded,
7 An RCD
8 A very small fault current

A protects people.
B it trips.
C more than a fuse.
D which breaks first.
E will trip an RCD.
F can be reset.
G be reset.
H it blows.

## 2 Household wiring systems

A typical task for an electrician is dealing with household wiring systems. Study the text and the diagram, and then compare the British and the German household wiring systems.

In many houses in Britain there are basically two circuits – a 30 amp ring circuit to power electrical equipment (e.g. a dishwasher) and a 5 amp lighting circuit. Some appliances also have their own circuit or are connected to an existing circuit with a spur and a switched fused connection unit (e.g. for an extractor fan or an electric shower). Each circuit has a circuit breaker in the consumer unit. In addition to this, British plugs have a 3, 5 or 13 amp cartridge fuse which blows if overloaded.

Safety devices in household wiring

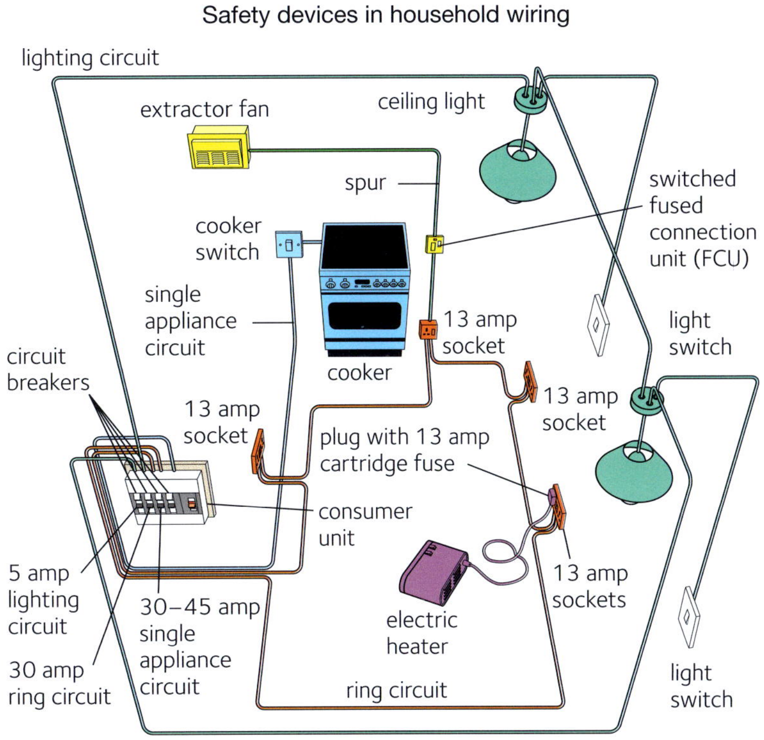


| | | |
|---|---|---|
| In British/German houses<br>A British/German electrician<br>In Britain/Germany, appliances<br>A British/German plug | there is/isn't | a circuit breaker for … |
| | there are/aren't | only two circuits. |
| | uses / doesn't use | a … amp … |
| | use / don't use | … amp circuit breakers. |
| | has / doesn't have | a separate switch for the … |
| | have / don't have | one big circuit breaker for … |

10

## 3 Wiring in an old pub

Sebastian Fischer is a German electrician on work placement in Britain. Today he's looking at the wiring in an old pub. Listen to the dialogue and then complete the following tasks.

1 Make a list of all the things that surprise him.
2 Say what you or your company would do to solve the problem in the pub.

**IT'S YOUR TURN**

Your boss wants you to draw a circuit diagram of the wiring in your own flat or house (or part of it). Do this and then give a presentation to the class explaining what safety features it has and how they work. Use the language box to prepare your presentation.

| |
|---|
| This diagram shows how … |
| Here we can see … |
| The purpose of an RCD / a fuse/ … is to protect appliances / prevent fires / … |
| Each circuit has/contains … |
| If the fuse blows / the circuit breaker trips, it can/can't be reset/replaced/… |
| If there is a fault current, … |

# 11 Safety rules

**This unit is about:**
- safe working practices
- safety signs at the workplace

**Competences:**
- explaining safety rules in English
- understanding English safety signs
- interpreting for an English-speaking colleague

## 1 Safety rules

Safety rules save lives. Choose the statements which correctly explain each of the five safety rules in German.

Rule no. 1: Before you work on electrical equipment or a circuit or you must
- a switch it off.
- b turn it off.
- c disconnect it.

Rule no. 2: The next thing you must do is
- a tell your workmates that you're working on the circuit or equipment.
- b lock and tag it so no one turns it back on again.
- c test the circuit to see if it's still live.

Rule no. 3: If, for example, the multimeter reading for the circuit is zero,
- a you still mustn't start work on it.
- b it's safe to start work on it.
- c you can be sure the circuit isn't live.

Rule no. 4: You short-circuit a circuit by
- a touching the black conductor against the blue conductor.
- b touching the blue conductor against the green-yellow conductor.
- c touching the black conductor against the green-yellow conductor.

Rule no. 5: If there are live electrical components near where you're working,
- a don't start work until you've disconnected them.
- b make it impossible to touch them if you can't disconnect them.
- c be careful not to touch them.

**5 SICHERHEITSREGELN**

Vor Beginn der Arbeiten:
- freischalten
- gegen Wiedereinschalten sichern
- Spannungsfreiheit feststellen
- erden und kurzschließen
- benachbarte, unter Spannung stehende Teile abdecken oder abschranken

## 2 Safety signs

★ a) What do these signs mean? Match the explanations with the signs.

A This equipment will not stop electrical equipment or installations from burning.
B There is no insulation on these conductors. If you touch them you will get a shock.
C You mustn't block this door because someone might need to open it quickly.
D Electricity enters this building underground, so you must be careful when using earth-moving machinery or tools.
E You mustn't switch this circuit back on again. Only the person who switched it off is allowed to switch it back on again.

1

2

3

4

5

| 1 | | 2 | | 3 | | 4 | | 5 | |
|---|---|---|---|---|---|---|---|---|---|

★★ b) Make a list of the signs you see at your workplace.

★★★ c) Write a short explanation of one of the signs in English.

## 3 Qualified electricians

Staying safe when on electrical installation is very important. Use the box to fill in the gaps. One gap has two possible answers.

must (2×) • is allowed to • mustn't (2×) • aren't allowed to (2×)

Only a qualified electrician ____________________ [1] do electrical installation work. If you aren't a qualified electrician, you ____________________ [2] work on a circuit. Even when you're qualified you ____________________ [3] always read the safety warnings before starting work. You also ____________________ [4] forget to switch off the circuit breaker and put a sign on the consumer unit. If you see a label on a circuit to say that another person has locked it out, you ____________________ [5] switch it back on again. You ____________________ [6] wait for that person to do so.

11

## 4 Interpreting for an English-speaking colleague

You are an apprentice electrician at Elektro Klein and today you have a British trainee called Alan Turner with you. You're about to work on an electrical circuit.

**Tip**
check = überprüfen/ kontrollieren

a) Before you start, explain to Alan what your foreman says about the safety rules. Work with two partners and role-play the dialogue. Use expressions like "He says that / He wants to know if…".

| Elektromeister | You | Alan |
| --- | --- | --- |
| 1 Was müsst ihr zuerst überprüfen, bevor ihr anfangt? | 2 He wants to know what … | 3 We should check to see if the circuit is live. |
| | 4 | |
| 5 Nicht schlecht, aber nicht richtig! | 6 | 7 OK, so what's the first step? |
| | 8 | |
| 9 Ihr müsst zuerst den Stromkreis freischalten. | 10 | 11 Ah yes, of course! Where do we disconnect it – at the consumer unit? |
| | 12 | |
| 13 Richtig! Könnt ihr jetzt mit der Arbeit anfangen? | 14 | 15 I don't think so. I think we should now check to see if the circuit is live. |
| | 16 | |
| 17 Noch nicht! Als Nächstes müsst ihr ein Schild an den Sicherungskasten hängen, damit niemand den Stromkreis wieder einschaltet. | 18 | 19 Yes, that makes sense. And after you've put the sign on the consumer unit, what's next? |

b) Now listen to the example dialogue and check how well you interpreted.

**IT'S YOUR TURN**
Work with a partner. One of you is the British trainee and the other is the apprentice electrician. Take it in turns to ask about and explain the last three safety rules to each other in English.

# 12 Electric lighting

**This unit is about:**
- commonly used sources of light
- energy efficiency and colour rendition
- the materials used in sources of light

**Competences:**
- understanding a spoken description
- describing and comparing sources of light
- giving a presentation about different sources of light

## 12 1 Electric lighting

Here are eight sources of light.

★ a) How many of these sources of light can you name? How energy-efficient do you think they are? Listen to the recording and check your answers.

| Light source | | Properties | Efficiency |
|---|---|---|---|
| A ______ |  Fotolia.com/puchan | produces yellow light; extremely energy-efficient; very long life | ____% |
| B ______ ______ | 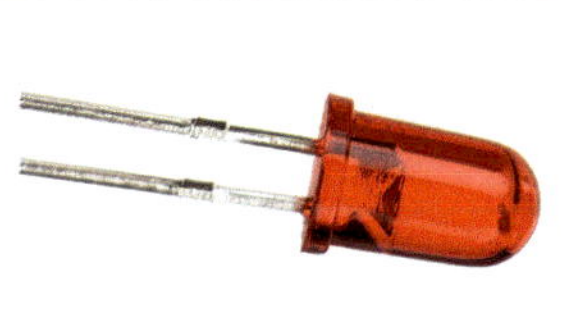 Shutterstock/Feng Yu | available in many colours; energy-efficient; doesn't get hot; long life; used in electronic equipment and for decoration; some types are expensive | ____% |
| C ______ ______ |  Fotolia.com/kaiskynet | energy-efficient; good colour rendition; contains mercury; expensive; not dimmable | ____% |
| D ______ |  Shutterstock/Fotos593 | energy-efficient; good colour rendition; long life; can produce ultra-violet light for medical and cosmetic use; contains mercury; expensive; not dimmable | ____% |
| E ______ |  Shutterstock/nubephoto | very powerful light; used for floodlights at sports stadiums; good colour rendition; takes several minutes to warm up or restart; can explode | ____% |
| F ______ |  Fotolia.com/Jultud | extremely intense light used in film projectors; must be water-cooled; gas is under high pressure; can explode | ____% |
| G ______ | 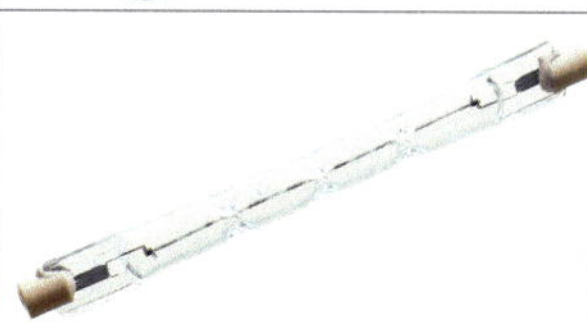 Shutterstock/vvoe | very bright light; dimmable; can be used inside, outside and in vehicles; can become very hot; bulb blows sooner if touched | ____% |
| H ______ ______ |  Fotolia.com/Gor Grigoryan | excellent colour rendition (produces warm, natural light); cheap to replace; dimmable; short life; highly inefficient | ____% |

★★ b) Select the right source of light (A–H) from opposite for the following uses.

1 an energy-saving ceiling light
2 a strip light for the kitchen
3 decorative lighting in a home
4 a powerful garden light
5 a street light
6 stadium floodlights
7 an old-style outdoor light
8 a film projector

| 1 | | 2 | | 3 | | 4 | | 5 | | 6 | | 7 | | 8 | |
|---|---|---|---|---|---|---|---|---|---|---|---|---|---|---|---|

★★★ c) Use the table to write sentences about the eight sources of light and their uses.

| | | | | | |
|---|---|---|---|---|---|
| A/An …<br>CFLs<br>LEDs<br>… | is/are<br>is/are often<br>is/are normally<br>is/are sometimes | used for<br>found in | projectors<br>car headlights<br>street lighting<br>floodlights | because it's/<br>they're | safe.<br>cheap/soft/bright.<br>efficient/attractive.<br>powerful.<br>economical/expensive. |

______________________________________________

______________________________________________

______________________________________________

______________________________________________

______________________________________________

______________________________________________

______________________________________________

______________________________________________

## 2 Sources of light

A customer wants to know about different types of light sources. Complete the sentences with a suitable comparison.

cheap • dangerous • efficient • expensive • long • soft

**Tip**

Short adjectives:
short – shorter than – (the) shortest
Long adjectives:
economical – more/less economical than – (the) most/least economical

1 LEDs only cost a few cents so they ______________________ CFLs.
2 A fluorescent tube is ______________ a halogen lamp but ______________ a sodium lamp.
3 Of all the light sources sodium lamps have ______________ life span.
4 Of all the light sources an incandescent bulb is ______________________.
5 The pressurized gas in a xenon short arc lamp makes it ______________________ a CFL.

**IT'S YOUR TURN**

As part of your training you should understand different sources of electric light. With a partner, list the sources in your a) classroom, b) own home and c) workplace. Give a presentation to the class on what you find and include the following factors:

colour • cost and efficiency • environmental dangers • safety

| |
|---|
| We now wish to present you the results of our energy survey. |
| We found that … |
| The following data/chart/graph/diagram shows that … |

# Extra practice: Units 9–12

## 1 Storing electrical energy

a) Label the four sources of electrical energy (1–4).

1
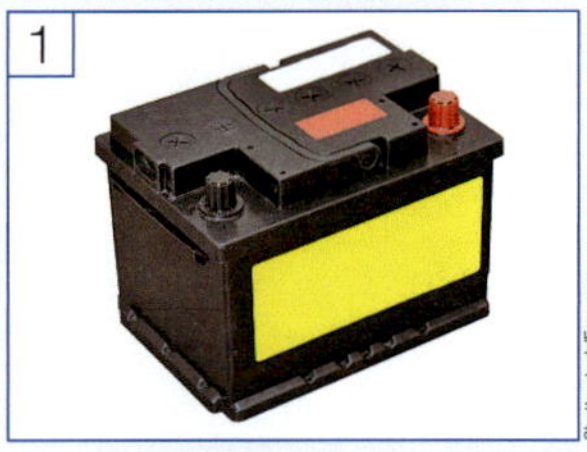
Shutterstock/Ensuper

_______________

2

Shutterstock/BravissimoS

_______________

3
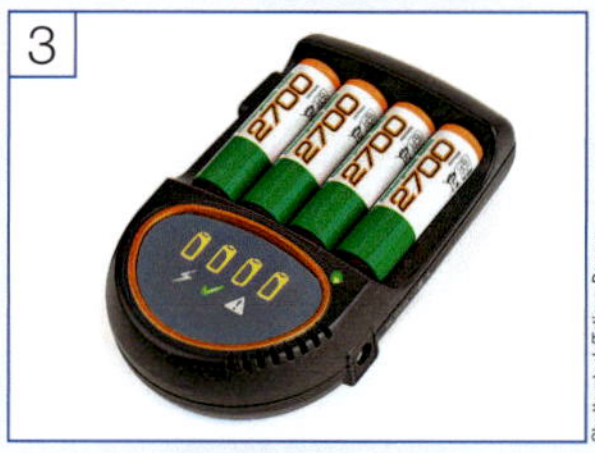

Shutterstock/Tatiana Popova

_______________

4
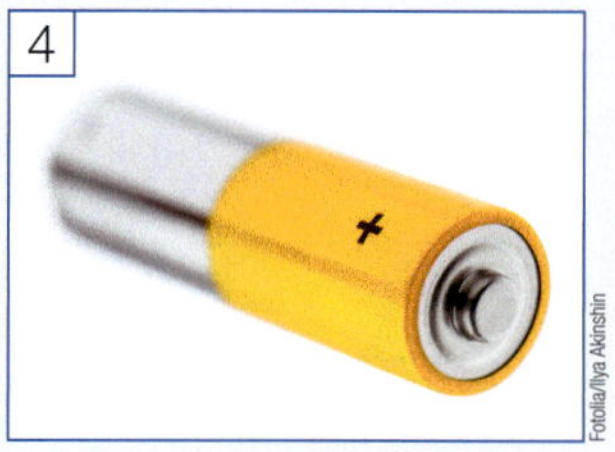

Fotolia/Ilya Akinshin

_______________

_______________

b) Which of the four electricity sources above is this a description of?

A small, cheap electrical component which is used to store a small charge, measured in farads (F), for a short time in an electrical circuit. The output in this case is 2.2 microfarads. ____

c) Write a short description of the other three sources of energy. Explain where and how they are used and add any extra information you may know, e.g. how long they last, their output, cost, advantages and disadvantages.

| | |
|---|---|
| 1 | car battery: |
| 2 | rechargeable battery: |
| 3 | non-rechargeable (single use) battery: |

## 2 Safety devices

You are a qualified electrician working with a Finnish apprentice called Martti Junkkari, who has come to your company for work experience. You are called to a house in which there is a smell of burning each time the tumble dryer is switched on, after which it trips the circuit breaker. You examine the socket and see the following (see photo).

Fotolia.com/anzebizjan

Explain in a few sentences what the problem is.

_______________

_______________

_______________

_______________

_______________

## 3 Electric lighting

a) Research on the Internet if necessary, then complete the table to show what type or types of lighting are best in the following situations and how efficient they are.

| Situation | Type(s) of lighting | Efficiency (%) |
|---|---|---|
| 1 a football stadium | | |
| 2 a laboratory | | |
| 3 an art gallery | | |
| 4 a motorway tunnel | | |
| 5 multi-coloured party lighting | | |

b) Choose one of your answers above (1–5) and explain in a few sentences why this type of lighting is best in the situation given.

## ▶▶▶ ICH KANN

| | | Seite/Übung |
|---|---|---|
| ☐ | Ich kann eine eingeübte, kurze und einfache Präsentation zu einem Thema vortragen, das mir vertraut ist. Ich kann dabei einfache Nachfragen beantworten, wenn ich um Wiederholung bitten kann. A2 | 31/ It's your turn |
| ☐ | Ich kann in einfachen zusammenhängenden Sätzen Diagramme beschreiben und interpretieren. B1 | 27/ It's your turn |
| ☐ | Ich kann berufs- oder fachbezogene Sachverhalte und Prozesse (z. B. Elektrizität, Kabelsysteme in Haushalten) einfach, aber strukturiert beschreiben, erklären bzw. zusammenfassen. B1 | 25/It's your turn; 27/2 |
| ☐ | Ich kann eine Rolle in einem Dialog oder einer Simulation übernehmen (z. B. Berufssituation). A2 | 29/4; 29/ It's your turn |
| ☐ | Ich kann kurzen und deutlich gesprochenen Texten und Tonträgern die wesentlichen Informationen entnehmen, wenn es um vorhersehbare alltägliche oder berufsspezifisch vertraute Dinge (z. B. Beschreibung von Elektrizität, Gleichstrom, *Lenz's Law*) geht. A2 | 27/3 |
| ☐ | Ich verstehe umfassende Anweisungen, Fragen, Auskünfte in beruflichen Situationen und auf Reisen. B1 | 30/1a |
| ☐ | Ich kann einfachen Alltagstexten, die sich auf vertraute Situationen beziehen, die wichtigsten Informationen entnehmen (z. B. berufliche Alltagsbeschreibungen, Gleich-/Wechselstrom, Sicherheitsbeschreibung). A2 | 28/1 |
| ☐ | Ich kann einfache Sachtexte (z. B. Beschreibung von Strom und Stromspannung) verstehen, wenn Bilder oder Grafiken den Inhalt unterstützen. A2 | 25/2; 25/3; 28/2a; 31/1b |
| ☐ | Ich kann Informationen in verschiedenen längeren Texten oder Textteilen finden, die ich brauche, um eine bestimmte Aufgabe zu lösen. B1 | 24/1a; 26/1a, b, c |
| ☐ | Ich kann Listen schreiben (z. B. Produktlisten) und einfache Formulare ausfüllen. A1 | 25/1c, 29/2b |
| ☐ | Ich kann einfache beschreibende Texte zu grundlegenden Sachverhalten oder Aufgabenstellungen aus meinem Fachgebiet (z. B. Sicherheitsschilder) verfassen. B1 | 29/2c |

# 13 DC motors

**This unit is about:**
- the properties of a magnetic field
- building a simple DC motor
- how a DC motor works

**Competences:**
- following spoken instructions
- following written instructions
- explaining a technical process step by step

## 13 1 How to build a DC motor in ten minutes

Learning how to build a DC motor is good practice for an electrician.

Put the instructions (A–J) in the same order as the photos, then listen to the recording and check your answer.

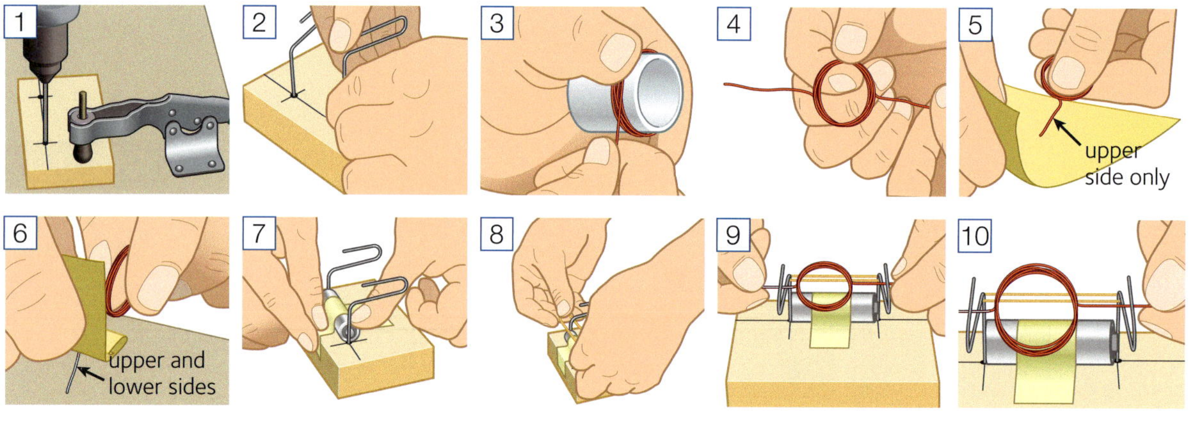


| Materials required |
| --- |
| an AA battery • a rubber band • two paper clips • a square magnet • a piece of plastic tube • 40 cm of insulated wire • a piece of fine sandpaper • a small block of wood |

A Bend open the two paper clips to form metal holders and insert them into the holes in the wooden base.
B Completely sand away 5 cm of the insulation from the other end of the wire.
C Drill two holes in the block of wood 5 cm apart (the length of an AA battery).
D Give the top of the coil a gentle push to start it turning. It will then spin alone.
E Leave 5 cm of wire free at each end and wrap the ends of the wire around the coil so they stick out exactly opposite each other.
F Place the rubber band around the paper clip holders so they press hard against the terminals of the battery.
G Place the two ends of the coil in the metal paper clip holders. Place the magnet under the coil.
H Sand away 5 cm of the insulation from the upper side of one end of the wire. The lower side of the wire remains insulated.
I Tape the battery to the wooden base so its ends touch the two paper clips.
J Wrap the wire around the plastic tube seven times to make a coil.

1 ___ 2 ___ 3 ___ 4 ___ 5 ___ 6 ___ 7 ___ 8 ___ 9 ___ 10 ___

## 2 DC motors

This text explains the technical background of a DC motor.

★ a) Read the text and then label the diagram with the words in blue.

In a DC motor there is a permanent magnet (stator) around an armature, which is a coil of wire wound around a piece of iron. The armature is mounted on an axle so it can turn freely. The magnet doesn't move. The armature is connected to a battery by brushes which press against one end of it. The current from the battery travels along the coil of wire and produces a magnetic field around the armature. When the north end of this field is next to the north end of the permanent magnet, the armature is repelled. The result is the rotation of the armature away from the permanent magnet's magnetic field. At this point the armature would normally stop, but it doesn't because the current enters it through the two plates of a split-ring commutator. After it has turned 180°, the armature changes polarity because the commutator reverses the direction of the current with each half-turn.

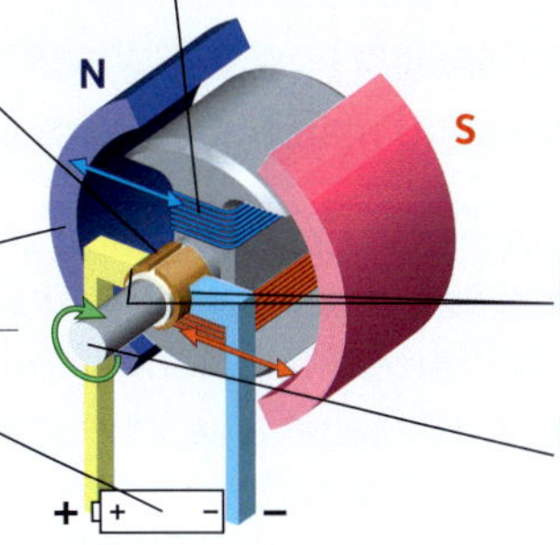


★★ b) Complete the sentences with words from the text.

1 A stator is ______________________________.

2 The armature can turn because ______________________________.

3 The current reaches the armature through ______________________________.

4 The north end of the permanent magnet repels ______________________________.

5 The brushes press against the plates ______________________________.

6 The function of the commutator is to ______________________________.

★★★ c) Use prepositions from the text to fill in the gaps.

If a DC motor only has an armature __________ [1] two poles, there are only two plates __________ [2] the commutator, so when the armature turns __________ [3] the axle, it comes __________ [4] a position where each commutator brush presses __________ [5] both commutator plates __________ [6] the same time, which produces a short circuit. In order to use the current __________ [7] the battery all the time, a DC motor usually has three or more poles. If a motor has a 3-pole armature, one __________ [8] its poles will always be repelled __________ [9] the stator's magnetic field __________ [10] any time, making it run more smoothly.

**IT'S YOUR TURN**

Use the Internet to find more examples of simple DC motors (e.g. with a nail). Find or draw diagrams which show the materials needed and how they are assembled. Present them to the class, explaining each step as you go.

| | |
|---|---|
| First/Then/Next / After that / Finally … | You have to do this (carefully/slowly/gently) because … |
| You make sure that … | |
| For this motor you'll need … | You can see that … |
| Take the … and bend/cut/… it. | This is because … |
| You use the tube/sandpaper to … | |

# 14 3-phase induction motor

**This unit is about:**
- how an AC induction motor works
- mains supply polarity
- the torque of an electric motor

**Competences:**
- understanding technical explanations
- recommending a suitable electric motor
- describing how an AC motor works

## 1 3-phase induction motors

The text below explains how a 3-phase induction motor works.

★ a) Read the text and match the words in blue with their German equivalents in the box.

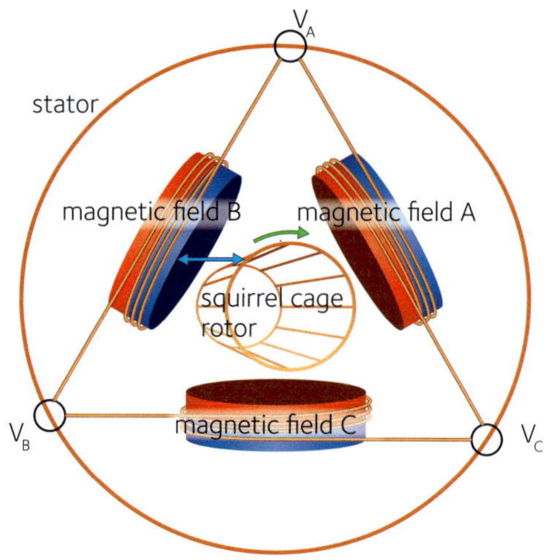


A 3-phase induction motor has a stator[1] in which there is a rotating magnetic field around a rotor. The rotating[2] magnetic field in the stator induces[3] a current in the copper rods[4] of the rotor. This current generates a second magnetic field around the rotor. In the diagram, the north polarity of the rotor is repelled[5] by the north polarity of magnetic field B, so the rotor turns away from it. At the same time, the north polarity of the rotor is attracted[6] by the south polarity of magnetic field A, so it turns towards it. This happens again and again as the rotor moves[7] through the magnetic fields. Magnetic fields A, B and C are produced by the three phases of the AC mains supply[8], which in Europe has a frequency of 50 Hertz, meaning it changes polarity 50 times per second. The speed at which the rotor turns is controlled by the number of magnetic fields in the stator and the frequency of the AC supply voltage, so a 3-phase induction motor will naturally reach one speed and stay at that speed. In the past, this was a major[9] disadvantage but nowadays[10] it is possible to use an electronic variable frequency drive (VFD) to regulate how often the magnetic fields change polarity and therefore the speed at which the rotor turns.

☐ abgestoßen • ☐ angezogen • ☐ groß • ☐ heutzutage • ☐ induziert • ☐ bewegt sich • ☐ sich drehend • ☐ Stäbe • ☐ Ständer • ☐ Stromnetz

★★ b) Use the text and the diagram to match the sentence halves.

1 There is a rotating magnetic field
2 The rotor is made of
3 A second magnetic field is generated
4 The north polarity in the stator
5 50 Hertz means that every second
6 How fast the rotor turns depends
7 Nowadays it's easier to
8 A VFD regulates how often

A the mains supply changes polarity fifty times.
B the AC mains supply changes polarity.
C control the speed of the motor.
D on two factors.
E around the rotor.
F in the stator.
G copper rods.
H repels the north polarity in the rotor.

★★★ c) Choose the right answer to complete the sentences.

1 In a 3-phase induction motor the stator a) moves all the time b) doesn't move at all c) sometimes moves.
2 The magnetic field a) only attracts the rotor b) only repels the rotor c) both attracts and repels the rotor.
3 When the north polarity of the rotor meets the north polarity of the magnetic field, the rotor a) stops b) turns away c) turns towards it.
4 If attached to a 60 Hertz AC mains supply (e.g. in the USA), this motor will turn a) faster b) more slowly c) at the same speed.

## 2 A crossword

Use words from the text to fill in the crossword.

**Across**

4 The alternating current in this motor has three … .

6 The opposite of 'repel' is … .

7 The magnetic … in the stator produces another one in the rotor.

8 The rotor is made of … .

10 The short form of 'alternating current' is … .

11 The … is the part of the motor which doesn't move.

12 A magnetic field which turns is a … magnetic field.

**Down**

1 The opposite of 'attract' is … .

2 In Europe alternating current has a … of 50 Hertz.

3 Something which you can change is … .

5 Frequency is measured in … .

9 If a magnetic field changes from north to south, it changes … .

14 

## 3 Ventilation systems

Jenny Green's company has just bought an office block in Leipzig. The building is over 50 years old and the ventilation system is inefficient, so Jenny has asked Andreas Ritter from Horstmeier Luft- und Klimatechnik GmbH to give her some advice.
Fill in the gaps with words from the recording.

1 Jenny and Andreas are on the ___________ of the building.

2 The ventilation system is just a big air shaft with a ___________ on it.

3 Andreas suggests installing a supply and a return ___________.

4 One will suck in fresh air and the other will ___________ stale air.

5 The motors will be AC ___________ motors.

6 By using a VFD you can ___________ the speed of the motor.

7 A VFD is _____________________ free.

8 The part of the motor which moves is the ___________ cage rotor.

9 Torque is the ___________ you need to turn something.

10 Andreas will send Jenny an ___________ in the next few days.

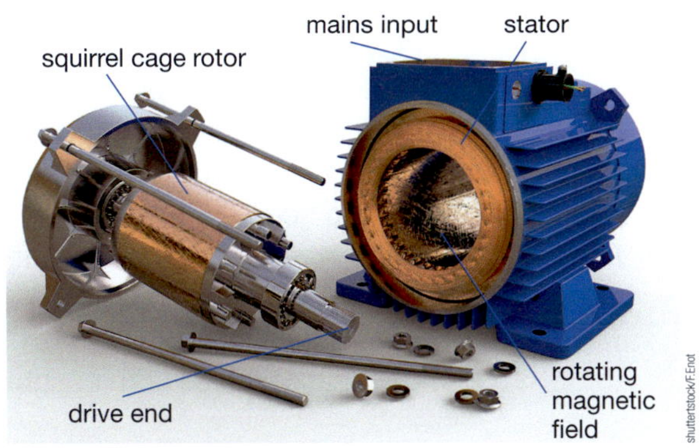


**IT'S YOUR TURN**

Work with a partner and give a short presentation explaining how the squirrel cage motor shown here works and the sort of situations it is used in. Use your electrical engineering textbook and the Internet for more information, if necessary.

# 15 Pure electric vehicles

**This unit is about:**
- frequently used AC and DC motors
- popular misconceptions about electric vehicles
- driving an electric vehicle

**Competences:**
- understanding a technical text and diagram
- listening to a radio interview
- describing an electric vehicle

## 1 Pure electric vehicles

Electric vehicles, EVs, use different types of electric motors, depending on the jobs they do. The oldest motor type is a DC motor with brushes. These have a permanent magnet around a rotating armature with windings. The armature is connected to a commutator. DC motors can also be brushless, and in such motors a permanent magnet rotates inside field coils on the outside of the motor. An encoder on the axle of the permanent magnet controls when the field magnets change polarity. In AC induction motors there is often a squirrel cage rotor made of windings or copper rods inside a stator with a rotating magnetic field.

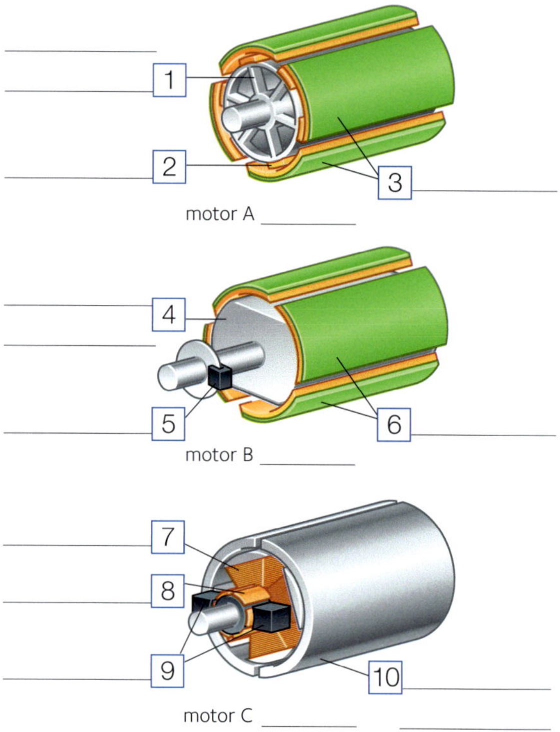


★ a) Study the text and find the English equivalents of the German words.

1 je nachdem ____________________
2 sich drehend ____________________
3 Windungen ____________________
4 verbunden mit ____________________
5 bürstenlos ____________________
6 Achse ____________________
7 Kupfer ____________________
8 Stäbe ____________________

★★ b) Read the text and label the diagram (points 1–10) with the words in blue. You will need one of the words twice.

★★★ c) Label the three diagrams AC or DC. Write a few sentences to explain how one of the motors works. Use the explanations in units 13 and 14.

15 ## 2 Trends in the car industry

Jane Riley is a reporter for *Top Gear*, a radio programme about trends in the car industry. Listen to her talking to Tom Bell, whose company makes electric cars. Use the dialogue to reply to the statements after it.

Jane: Hello and welcome to *Top Gear*. Today I'm talking to Tom Bell about EVs, and if you're not quite sure what that means, an EV is an electric vehicle. Why should I buy an EV, Tom?

Tom: There are so many reasons I just don't know where to start, so I suggest you come for a test drive in one of our electric sports cars. We can talk while we're driving.

Jane: Won't it be too noisy?

Tom: Let's find out, shall we? Here's the car. Would you like to get in? Please fasten your seat belt. And off we go!

Jane: Wow, it's really fast! It's like a Formula 1 racing car!

Tom: That's right. It accelerates from nought to 60 miles per hour in just four seconds. And did you hear any noise?

Jane: There was none at all! It's like a ghost!
Tom: Exactly. This is a pure electric car. It's so quiet that you can drive it at night without waking people up, and it also has zero emissions.
Jane: That's great news for the environment, Tom, but how come it's so fast?
Tom: Electric motors have very high power even at low speeds, which means you can accelerate very quickly. This car will actually do 125 mph. And you don't need to change gear in this vehicle because there's no gearbox. It drives like an automatic.
Jane: Well that certainly does make things a lot easier! Now where does all this power come from?
Tom: It's from the lithium-ion battery pack behind our seats. Let's just stop here and I'll show you. Let's get out and look at the back of the car. You just plug the power cord into this socket here to recharge the batteries.
Jane: But where can you recharge them and how long does it take? You can't just go to a petrol station, can you?
Tom: Not yet, but you soon will! When you buy this car you get a home charging station, which we install in your garage, so you can recharge the batteries in three and a half hours. Most people do this overnight. And soon there'll be a network of charging stations all over the country. There's just one more thing I think I should tell your listeners, Jane. This car has regenerative braking, which means that when it slows down the motor actually recharges the battery, so it's about 90% efficient.
Jane: This is very clever stuff! And what about the range?
Tom: It has a range of 200 miles, which is about 320 km, per battery charge.
Jane: And the price?
Tom: About $100,000, which is what you'd pay for a Porsche or a BMW.

1 EVs are slow! ______________________

2 EVs are noisy and pollute the environment! ______________________

3 EVs are hard to drive! ______________________

4 The battery takes all night to recharge! ______________________

5 EVs waste energy! ______________________

______________________

6 EVs have a very short range! ______________________

### IT'S YOUR TURN

You are working as a salesperson selling EVs at a car show. With a partner, write and act out a sales dialogue between yourself and a customer. Take it in turns to play each role.

| Customer | Salesperson |
| --- | --- |
| Sie fragen den/die Verkäufer/in, ob das ein Elektroauto ist. | Ja, das stimmt! Es ist ein rein elektrisch betriebenes Fahrzeug und hat Lithium-Ionen-Batterien. |
| Sie haben gehört, dass elektrische Fahrzeuge langsam sind. | Sie waren langsam, aber jetzt sind sie viel schneller. |
| Wie ist die Beschleunigung? | Dieser Sportwagen beschleunigt auf Tempo 100 in vier Sekunden. |
| Das ist sehr schnell! Stimmt es, dass man die Batterien jeden Tag über Nacht aufladen muss? | Das stimmt nicht! Man hat eine Reichweite von 320 km pro Ladung, also kann man lange fahren, ohne die Batterien aufzuladen. |
| Wie ist die Batterieladezeit? | Man braucht dreieinhalb Stunden, um die Batterien aufzuladen. |
| Wo kann man die Batterie aufladen? | Wenn man dieses Fahrzeug kauft, bekommt man auch eine Ladestation für zu Hause, aber bald wird es ein Netz von Ladestationen geben. |

# 16 Hybrid vehicles

**This unit is about:**
- vehicles using both electricity and petrol
- regenerative braking
- the pros and cons of hybrid vehicles

**Competences:**
- understanding a technical text and diagram
- talking about hybrid vehicles
- supporting an opinion with technical data

## 1 Hybrid vehicles

★ a) How do hybrid vehicles work? Read the text and label the diagrams with the condition they show.

acceleration • low speed • regenerative braking • stationary

A hybrid vehicle has two sources of power – an internal combustion engine (ICE) and an electric motor. The wheels can be driven by the engine, the motor or both at the same time. An ICE has high torque at high speeds but low torque at low speeds and therefore wastes a lot of energy when the vehicle is stationary or moves off. An electric motor has maximum torque the moment it starts to turn, so it is ideally suited to power a vehicle from rest. In a hybrid vehicle, a computer with an energy monitoring function calculates the best energy source at any time and switches the engine and the motor on and off, as necessary. At the traffic lights, for example, when the vehicle is stationary, the ICE and the electric motor are switched off, so no power is wasted. However, as soon as the driver accelerates from a lower to a higher speed, the ICE kicks in and the vehicle is driven by both power sources. At low speeds (e.g. up to 70–80 km/h) when the vehicle isn't accelerating, only the electric motor is needed to turn the wheels. When the vehicle slows down or the driver puts the brakes on, very little power is lost because the energy which is not needed to turn the wheels is used to power a generator which recharges the battery. This is called regenerative braking.

1
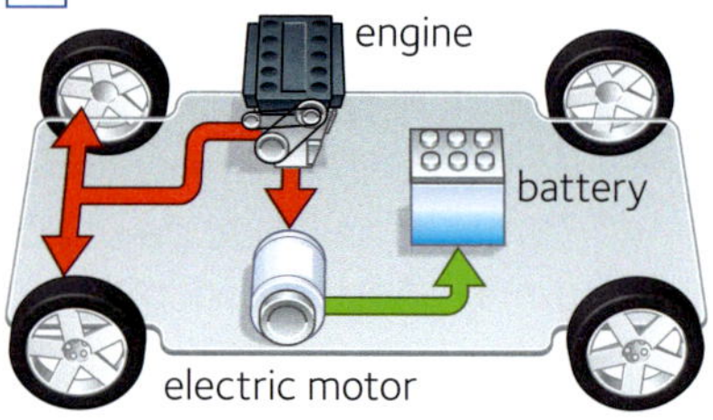


______________________

2
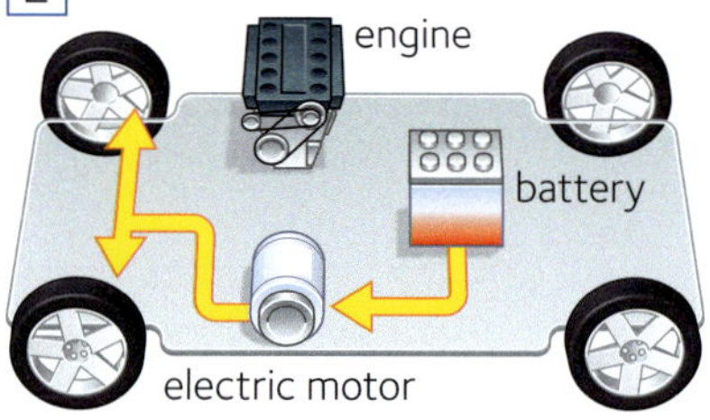


______________________

3
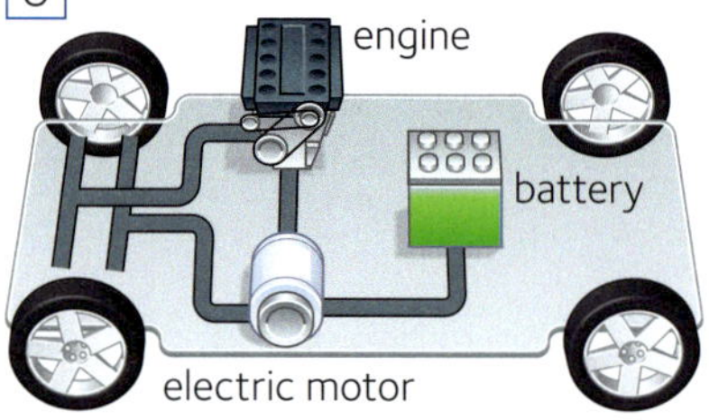


______________________

4
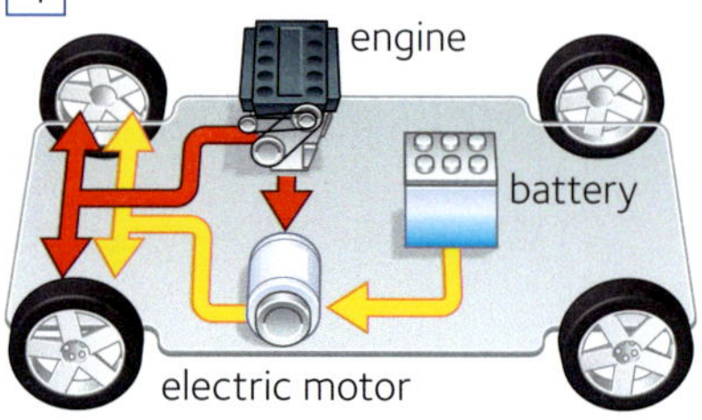


______________________

★★ b) Choose the right word to complete the sentences.

| 1 | The wheels of a hybrid vehicle are |
|---|---|
| a | always driven by one power source. |
| b | always driven by two power sources. |
| c | sometimes driven by two power sources. |

| 2 | An ICE is more efficient at |
|---|---|
| a | low speeds. |
| b | high speeds. |
| c | all speeds. |

| 3 | An electric motor |
|---|---|
| a | has full power at low speeds. |
| b | only has full power at low speeds. |
| c | only has full power at high speeds. |

| 4 | The computer switches on a hybrid's petrol engine |
|---|---|
| a | when the car speeds up quickly. |
| b | when the car is stationary. |
| c | at low speeds. |

★★★ c) Use words from the text to fill in the gaps.

The oldest ____________[1] vehicle on the market is the Toyota Prius. It has both an electric motor and a petrol ____________[2]. The motor has high ____________[3] at low speeds, so when the car ____________[4] off, the electric motor is the ____________[5] of power. This system is very efficient and little power is ____________[6]. However, as soon as the car ____________[7], the petrol engine ____________[8] in but when the vehicle slows down again the ____________[9] braking system ____________[10] the battery.

## 2 Discussing hybrid vehicles

**The taxi drivers' comments on this Internet discussion forum are mixed up. There are three statements and three reactions to these statements. Re-arrange the comments in logical pairs.**

| Tip |
|---|
| *BE*: petrol<br>*AE*: gasoline |

This month we're sharing our thoughts about hybrid taxis. Tell us what's on your mind!

| | |
|---|---|
| A | Those hi-tech nickel-metal hydride batteries in hybrids cost between \$5,000 – \$10,000! Are you prepared to spend all that money on just one car component? And isn't nickel a heavy metal?<br>*Nancy, San Antonio, Texas, USA* |
| B | The temperature is sometimes well below zero here, but I still drove 300,000 miles on my hybrid's original battery. I'm not planning to change to a regular cab. No way!<br>*Andrew, Vancouver, BC, Canada* |
| C | I agree that electricity is a clean and quiet source of energy, but think of how it's generated! What fuel does your power station use? If it's coal-fired, we're back to where we started.<br>*Fiona, Edinburgh, UK* |
| D | Why has no one mentioned the environment? Hybrids are so quiet you can't hear them at all when they're stationary. Their fuel consumption is only about 4 litres per 100 kilometres, and they emit as little as 93 g/km of $CO_2$. These facts speak for themselves.<br>*Tom, London, UK* |
| E | You get your money back in no time at all! Here in San Francisco we have calculated that averaging 90,000 miles per year, each cab saves \$9,000 on gasoline.<br>*Don, San Francisco, California, USA* |
| F | Why is everyone talking about electric motors? Anyone who did physics at school knows that a battery loses its power when it gets cold. Have you thought about that?<br>*Rashid, Accra, India* |

**IT'S YOUR TURN**

One day, you may have a job that involves hybrid vehicles. With a partner, make a list of the advantages and disadvantages of such vehicles. Add your own ideas and then say why you would or wouldn't buy a hybrid. Present your findings to the class and, after everybody has been heard, take a vote to find out how many are for and against hybrids. What is the majority opinion?

# Extra practice: Units 13–16

## 1 Electric motor quiz

A good way to revise what you have learned is to do a quiz. Find the right answers in this quiz.

| | |
|---|---|
| 1 | In an electric motor the stator |
| a | always moves. |
| b | never moves. |
| c | sometimes moves. |
| 2 | In an electric motor the rotor |
| a | always moves. |
| b | never moves. |
| c | sometimes moves. |
| 3 | In an electric motor the armature |
| a | always moves. |
| b | never moves. |
| c | sometimes moves. |
| 4 | In a DC motor the permanent magnet |
| a | always moves. |
| b | never moves. |
| c | sometimes moves. |
| 5 | In an electric motor the split-ring commutator changes |
| a | DC to AC electronically. |
| b | AC to DC electronically. |
| c | DC to AC mechanically. |
| 6 | A 3-phase induction motor has a rotating |
| a | stator. |
| b | armature. |
| c | magnetic field. |
| 7 | A 3-phase induction motor has |
| a | one magnetic field. |
| b | two magnetic fields. |
| c | three magnetic fields. |
| 8 | Opposite magnetic polarities |
| a | attract each other. |
| b | repel each other. |
| c | cancel each other out. |

| | |
|---|---|
| 9 | EVs |
| a | are quieter than cars with an ICE. |
| b | are noisier than cars with an ICE. |
| c | make as much noise as a car with an ICE. |
| 10 | An EV |
| a | only has high torque at high speeds. |
| b | only has high torque at low speeds. |
| c | has high torque at all speeds. |
| 11 | High torque at low speeds |
| a | is good for acceleration. |
| b | is bad for acceleration. |
| c | makes no difference to acceleration. |
| 12 | The batteries in an EV take |
| a | a day to recharge. |
| b | a few hours to recharge. |
| c | an hour to recharge. |
| 13 | In a hybrid vehicle |
| a | the ICE is used at low speeds. |
| b | both power sources are used at low speeds. |
| c | the electric motor is used at low speeds. |
| 14 | An ICE |
| a | has most torque at low speeds. |
| b | has most torque at high speeds. |
| c | has the same torque at all speeds. |
| 15 | In a hybrid vehicle the power source used is chosen |
| a | before the trip by the driver. |
| b | during the trip by a computer. |
| c | during the trip by the driver. |
| 16 | Regenerative braking means |
| a | the vehicle's brakes never wear out. |
| b | the motor which powers the wheels is reversed to recharge the battery. |
| c | the battery is switched off when the vehicle brakes. |

## 2 How an electric motor works

Do you know how an electric motor works?

★ a) Name parts 1–4 of the universal motor in the electric drill.

1 ____________________ 3 ____________________

2 ____________________ 4 ____________________

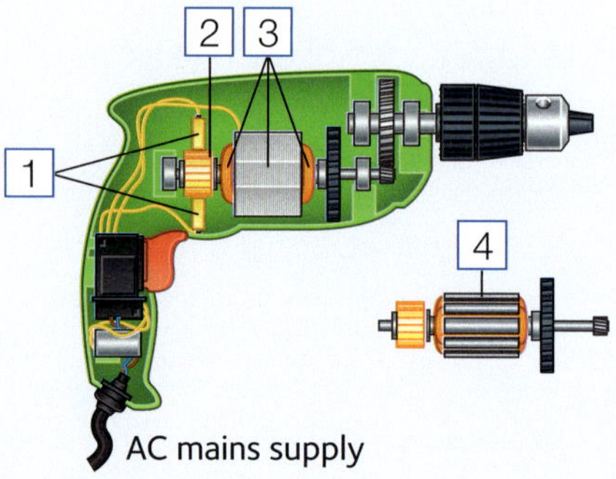

★★ b) Explain the function of each part of an electric motor.

★★★ c) Write a few sentences to explain how this universal motor works. Use your own knowledge, your textbook and/or the Internet to explain why the drill has an electromagnetic stator and not a permanent magnet.

## 3 Using a hybrid vehicle

The driver of a hybrid vehicle starts the car, drives off slowly, comes to a motorway and speeds up to 120 km/h, slows down, leaves the motorway, drives though a residential area, arrives home and parks the car. Choose one of the diagrams below for each part of the journey. Write the number of the diagram and what the car is doing each time.

1
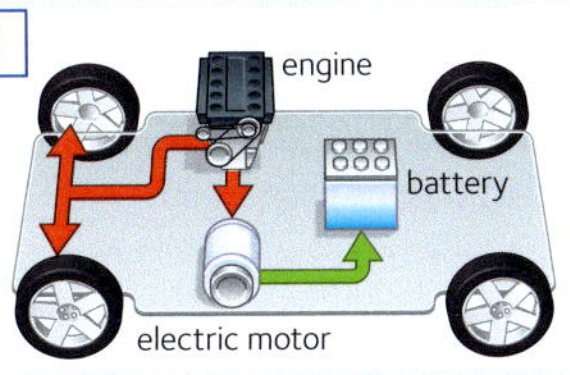


2
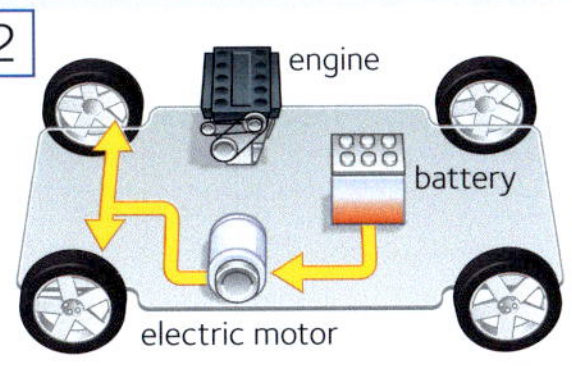


3
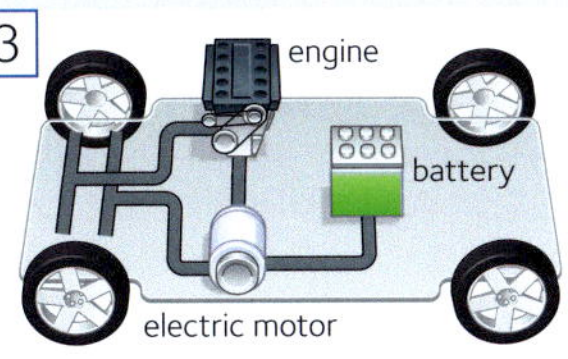


4
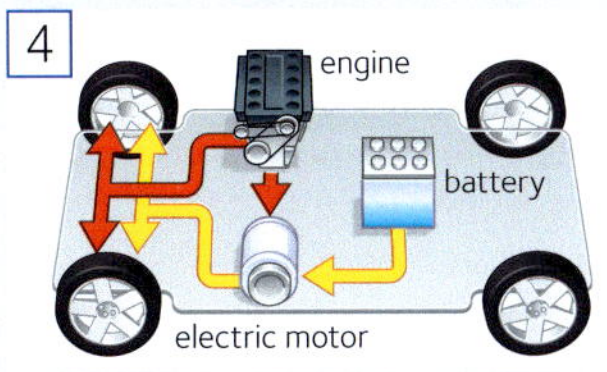


## ▶▶▶ ICH KANN

| | Seite/Übung |
|---|---|
| ☐ Ich kann in einfachen zusammenhängenden Sätzen Diagramme beschreiben und interpretieren. B1 | 25/ It's your turn |
| ☐ Ich kann eine Rolle in einem Dialog oder einer Simulation übernehmen (z. B. Berufssituation). A2 | 39/ It's your turn |
| ☐ Ich kann kurzen und deutlich gesprochenen Texten und Tonträgern die wesentlichen Informationen entnehmen, wenn es um vorhersehbare alltägliche oder berufsspezifisch vertraute Dinge (z. B. Beschreibung von Elektrizität, Gleichstrom, *Lenz's Law*) geht. A2 | 37/3 |
| ☐ Ich kann Anweisungen, Fragen und Auskünfte in Alltags-, Ausbildungs- und Berufssituationen im Wesentlichen verstehen. A2 | 34/1 |
| ☐ Ich verstehe das Wichtigste von Radiosendungen und Tonaufnahmen, wenn sie aktuelle Ereignisse oder meine Interessen betreffen. B1 | 38/2 |
| ☐ Ich kann einfachen Alltagstexten, die sich auf vertraute Situationen beziehen, die wichtigsten Informationen entnehmen (z. B. berufliche Alltagsbeschreibungen, Gleich-/Wechselstrom, Sicherheitsbeschreibung). A2 | 36/1a; 38/1a |
| ☐ Ich kann einfache Sachtexte (z. B. Beschreibung von Strom und Stromspannung) verstehen, wenn Bilder oder Grafiken den Inhalt unterstützen. A2 | 35/2a, b, c; 38/1b |
| ☐ Ich kann einfache Meldungen und Texte im Internet, in Computerprogrammen oder Computerspielen verstehen. A2 | 41/2 |
| ☐ Ich kann Informationen in verschiedenen längeren Texten oder Textteilen finden, die ich brauche, um eine bestimmte Aufgabe zu lösen. B1 | 36/1b, c; 40/1a, b, c |
| ☐ Ich kann Listen schreiben (z. B. Produktlisten) und einfache Formulare ausfüllen. A1 | 41/ It's your turn |
| ☐ Ich kann einfache beschreibende Texte zu grundlegenden Sachverhalten oder Aufgabenstellungen aus meinem Fachgebiet (z. B. Sicherheitsschilder) verfassen. B1 | 38/1c |

# 17 Electromagnetic control of currents

**This unit is about:**
- contactors
- relays
- troubleshooting

**Competences:**
- understanding a text about contactors
- listening to a recording
- explaining a schematic

## 1 Contactors

★ a) Study the text about contactors and find the English equivalents of the German words.

1 Schütz ______________ 2 Drehstrommotor ______________ 3 sich bewegen ______________
4 Kern ______________ 5 berühren ______________ 6 auseinander ______________

★★ b) Label the diagram of a contactor with the words in blue. You will need one of the words twice.

A contactor is an electromagnetic switch. It uses a low current to switch on a more powerful current, e.g. to operate a 3-phase induction motor. In a contactor, a control circuit energizes the contactor's coils which produce a magnetic field in the core. The magnetic field makes the armature move towards the contactor's core and when the armature moves, its two movable contacts touch the stationary contacts of the power circuit, which is then completed. A contactor has normally open (N/O) contacts because they are held apart by springs as long as there is no magnetic field.

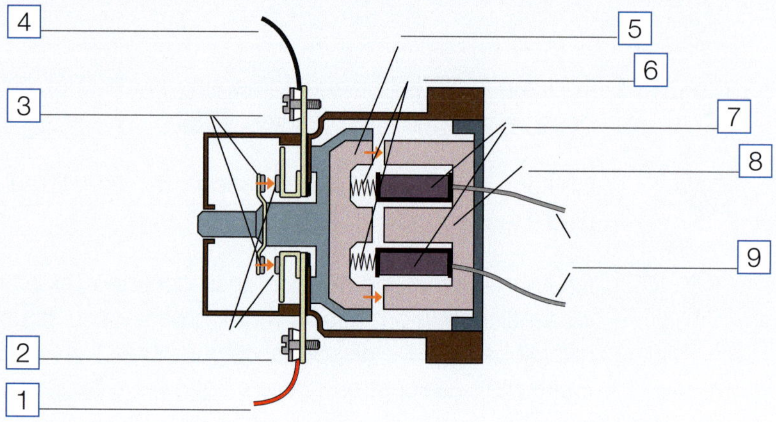


★★★ c) Match the sentence halves.

1 A contactor uses a low current
2 The low current produces
3 The magnetic field is in
4 The power circuit is completed

A the core of the contactor.
B when the armature moves.
C a magnetic field.
D to control a high current.

16 ## 2 How to install a car relay

An electrician is explaining how the five pins of a car relay for fog lights are connected. Complete the table below as you listen.

| Position of pin | Function | Number |
|---|---|---|
| | | |

## 3 Relay functions

Relays are important in the day-to-day work of an electrician. Use the table below to explain what happens when voltage is applied to relays 1 and 2.

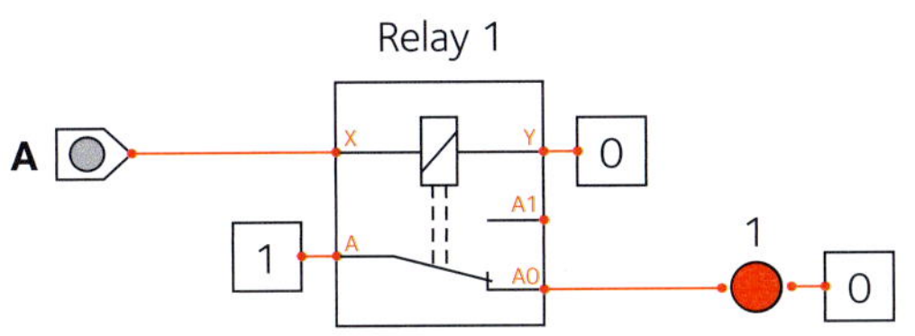


contact normally closed

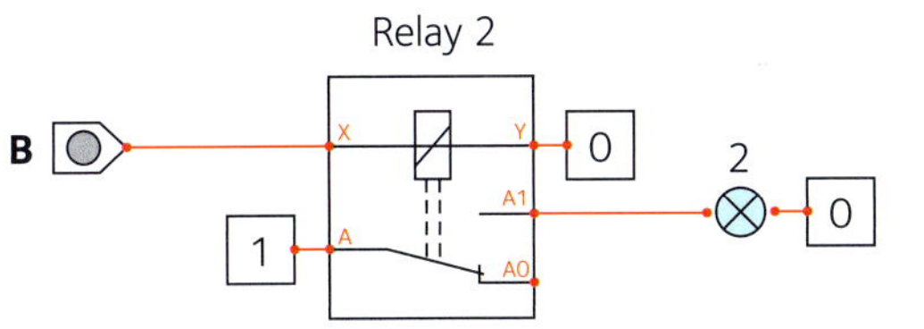


contact normally open

| | | | | | |
|---|---|---|---|---|---|
| When relay 1/2 | is activated by | switch A/B/…, | light bulb 1/2 | is | switched on/off. |
| | | both switches, | light bulbs … and … | are | |

17

## 4 Troubleshooting

A German electrician and a Finnish work placement student are looking at a problem with a conveyor belt in a warehouse.

a) Listen to the dialogue and fill in the gaps.

1 The conveyor belt keeps on ______________.

2 The conveyor belt has a separate switching unit with a ______________.

3 Martin and Lari have got a ______________ diagram.

4 It's a ______________ induction motor.

5 Lari thinks that one of the fuses has ______________.

6 With a contactor you can use a ______________ current to control a circuit with a high current.

7 The word they can see on the contactor is "__________".

8 The contactor has a motor ______________ function.

9 The overload heater contacts are normally ______________.

10 The motor is overheating because it hasn't been ______________ for years.

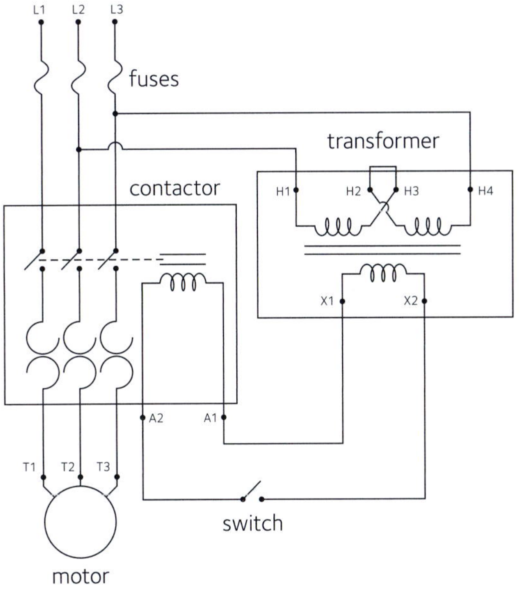


**Tip**

attract vs repel
switch on vs switch off

b) Use the expressions in the box to write a description of the schematic diagram in exercise a).

| | |
|---|---|
| It consists of … | The current in the … is higher/lower than the current in … |
| It is made up of … | The contacts in the … are normally open/closed. |
| The current enters the … | When the switch is thrown, the coil … |
| The current passes through the … | When the switching circuit is completed, … |
| The contactor gets its current from … | If the overload heaters trip, they … |

**IT'S YOUR TURN**

During your training you are asked to prepare a short presentation of another circuit (e.g. from your German electrical engineering textbook). Work with a partner and give the presentation to the class.

# 18 Electronic control of currents

**This unit is about:**

- semiconductors
- the electrical symbols for semiconductors
- p-n junctions

**Competences:**

- understanding how semiconductors work
- choosing a suitable semiconductor
- understanding a spoken explanation

## 1 Electronic control of currents

As an electrician you need to know about the components used in electronic circuits.

★ a) Use the words in blue in the text to label the diagrams below.

Electronic circuits need components for rectifying, switching, blocking, diverting and amplifying currents. These components are called semiconductors and are often made of silicon mixed with other elements which make the silicon positively or negatively charged. Positively charged silicon is called p-type silicon and negatively charged is called n-type. In some electrical circuits the current has to flow in one direction only and the current flowing in the opposite direction has to be blocked. To do this a diode made of one layer of p-type and one of n-type silicon is used. The point where the two layers meet is called the junction. A transistor uses p- and n-type silicon to make a low current or voltage amplify, switch or control a stronger current. In a bipolar junction transistor there are three layers of silicon separated by two junctions. A small current in the middle layer is used to control the much stronger current in the other two layers. In a field effect transistor there is p- and n-type silicon but one type is wrapped around the other. A low voltage in the outer layer is used to control how much current passes through the central channel of silicon. A component with four layers of silicon called a thyristor is used to switch very high currents.

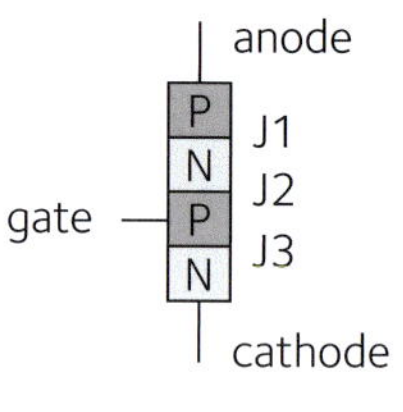


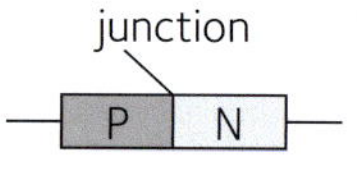


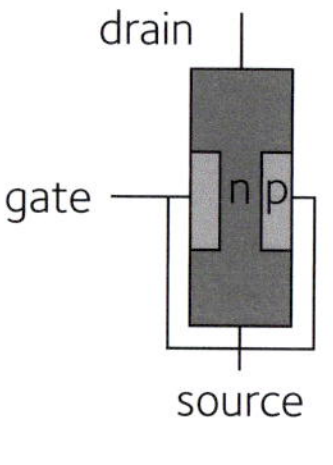


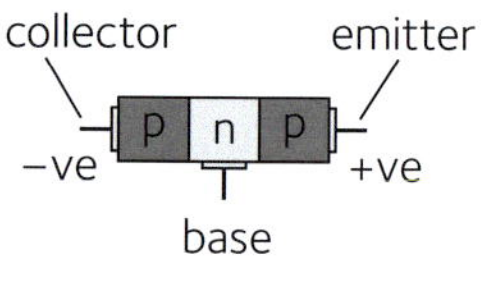


1 ______ 2 ______ 3 ______ 4 ______

★★ b) Use information from the text above to fill in the gaps.

Silicon is used in ______ [1] and is ______ [2] with other elements to produce ______ [3] types of silicon. In a diode two ______ [4] of silicon meet at a junction. A bipolar transistor has ______ [5] junctions. In a ______ [6] effect transistor there is a central ______ [7] through which the current passes. Very high currents are switched by a ______ [8], which has ______ [9] layers of silicon.

★★★ c) Use your electrical engineering textbook to match the symbols with the names.

bipolar junction transistor • diode • field effect transistor • thyristor

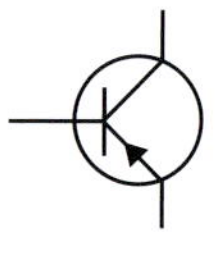

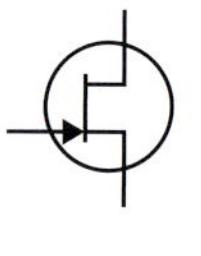

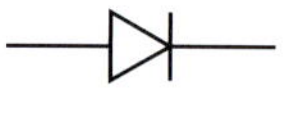

1 ______ 2 ______ 3 ______ 4 ______

## 2 A schematic

Electricians need to understand schematics.

★ a) Work with a partner and locate and name the components listed below.

Example: *Where's the capacitor? It's in square ... (e.g. E/F3).*

bridge rectifier ____________
capacitor ____________
diode(s) ____________
fuse(s) ____________
resistor(s) ____________
transformer ____________
transistor ____________
Zener diode ____________

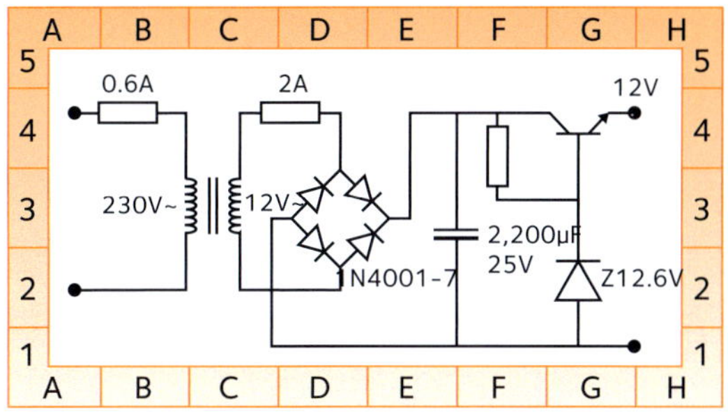


★★ b) Write a sentence explaining what each component in the above circuit does.

| | | |
|---|---|---|
| A capacitor | amplifies | a component. |
| A diode | blocks | a current. |
| A fuse | limits | a current up and down. |
| A transformer | protects | an electric charge. |
| A resistor | rectifies | an overcurrent. |
| A transistor | smooths | a signal. |
| | steps | |
| | stops | |
| | stores | |
| | switches | |

18

## 3 Components of a circuit

What is the schematic above for? Listen to the dialogue in which an apprentice electrician (Jason) asks a colleague (Brian) for help with a schematic. Fill in the table as you listen.

| Correct component | Type | Maximum rating |
|---|---|---|
| Diode | | |
| Transistor | | |
| Function of the circuit | | |

19

**IT'S YOUR TURN**

What is this schematic for? Brian explains another schematic to Jason.

If you already know what the schematic is for, write down your answer and hide it. Later, after you have listened to the recording, compare it with other students' answers. Were you right?

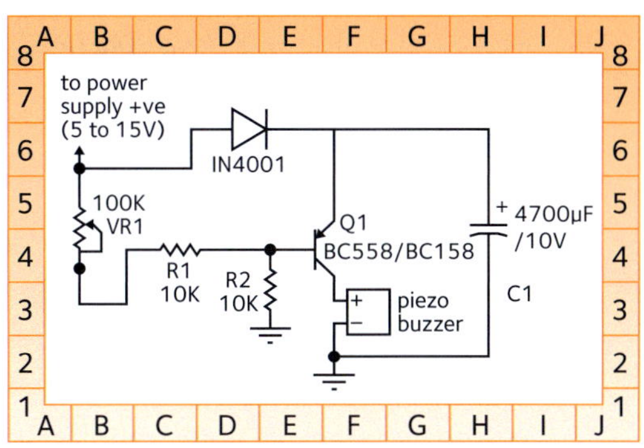

# 19 Control systems

**This unit is about:**
- open and closed loop control systems
- continuous and discontinuous action controllers

**Competences:**
- understanding a technical text
- identifying different control systems
- obtaining and presenting information

## 1 Open and closed loop control systems

Electricians need to know about control systems in their daily work.

★ a) Study the text and find the English equivalents of the German words.

1 Kippschalter ____________________
2 Schaltkreis ____________________
3 durchbrennen ____________________
4 gewünscht ____________________
5 unterbrochen ____________________
6 kontinuierlich ____________________
7 Streifen ____________________
8 Ventil ____________________
9 Steuerung ____________________
10 Regelkreis ____________________

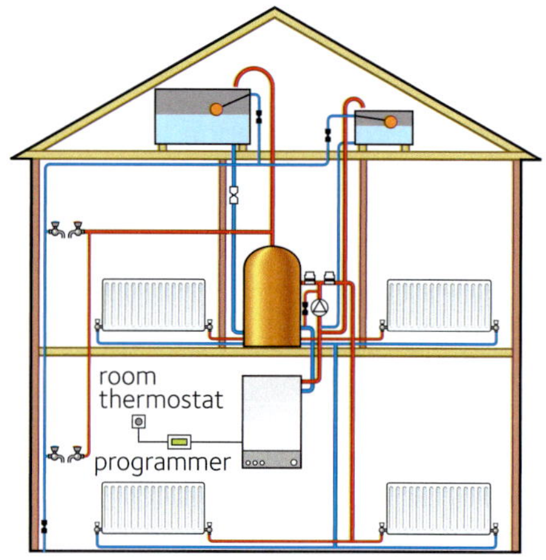


★★ b) Read the text and match the sentence halves.

The simplest control system is a toggle switch, which is either on or off. In a simple lighting circuit the switch completes the circuit and turns the light bulb on. There is no feedback to the switch to break the circuit if, for example, the light is too bright or the bulb blows. This is an example of an open loop control system. However, a typical central heating system works on a different principle. The householder selects a temperature, the system switches the heater on until the desired temperature is reached and then there is feedback to the system which switches the heater off again. When the temperature becomes too low, there is more feedback to the switch to turn the heater back on again. This type of system is called a closed loop control system. A closed loop control system can have a discontinuous or a continuous action controller. In the case of an electric iron, for example, a bimetallic strip makes or breaks the circuit depending on the temperature of the iron. This type of control system is inexact and slow and is an example of a two-position, discontinuous action controller. If, however, the temperature of a liquid in a steam-heated tank is to be kept absolutely constant, a different system is needed. In such cases a sensor continuously registers the temperature of the liquid and sends signals back to the motor operating the valve to let more, less or no steam in. In this way the temperature stays constant. This is an example of a continuous action controller.

1 An on/off switch is an example of
2 An open loop control system isn't
3 An open loop control system
4 A closed loop control system
5 A discontinuous action controller reacts
6 A continuous action controller uses
7 Continuous action control is more
8 The temperature in a two-position closed loop temperature control system

A is always between a maximum and minimum value.
B slowly.
C exact than a discontinuous action control.
D constant feedback.
E an open loop controller.
F always uses feedback.
G normally used in a central heating system.
H never uses feedback.

★★★ c) Open or closed loop? Put these devices in the right columns below.

bimetallic strip • contactor • cruise control • dimmer • driverless car • relay • thermostat • washing machine programme switch

| open loop | closed loop |
| --- | --- |
| | |

## 2 Closed loop control: mercury switch

It is important to know about mercury switches. Read the text and then label the parts of the mercury switch with the words in blue.

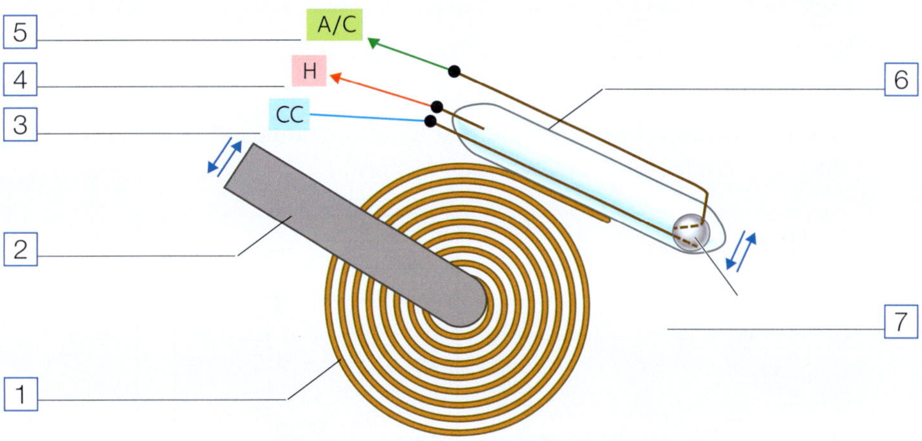


The mercury switch in the diagram switches a heater on and an air conditioner off. It is made of a glass vial which has a common contact at the bottom running from left to right. At the moment this contact is connected by a small quantity of mercury to the wire leading to the air conditioner. The vial is attached to a thermometer coil with a lever in the middle. The coil is a bimetallic strip. If the temperature now goes down, the bimetallic strip will contract, the glass vial will tip to the left and the mercury will run to the left, switch off the air conditioner and switch on the heater.

20

## 3 Cruise control systems

An instructor is explaining to a trainee how a cruise control system works. Listen to the description and complete the list.

1 ______________________
2 ______________________
3 ______________________
4 ______________________
5 ______________________
6 ______________________
7 ______________________
8 ______________________
9 ______________________

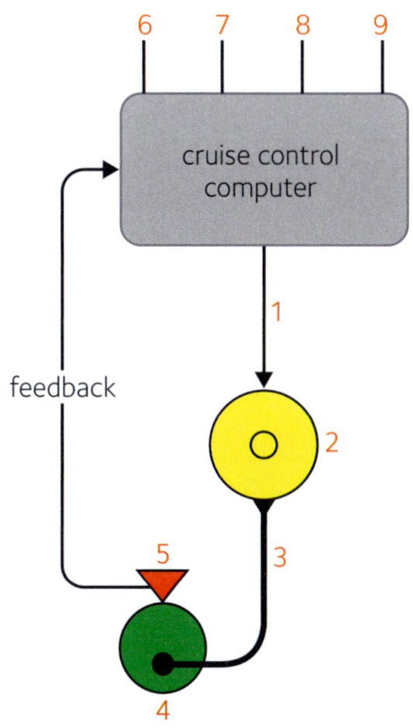


**IT'S YOUR TURN**

With a partner research on the Internet to find out how a driverless car operates, then give a presentation to your class.

# 20 Sensors

**This unit is about:**
- different types of sensors
- the industrial use of sensors
- PLCs

**Competences:**
- understanding a technical text and diagram
- understanding how sensors and PLCs are used
- taking visitors on a guided tour of a factory

## 1 Sensors

Today, sensors are used everywhere.

★ a) Study the text and find the English equivalents of the German words.

1 speicherprogrammierbare Steuerung ______ 2 regeln ______
3 Förderband ______ 4 erkennen ______
5 Druck ______ 6 Stau ______

★★ b) Use the words in blue from the text to label points 1–8 in the diagram of a factory conveyor belt system.

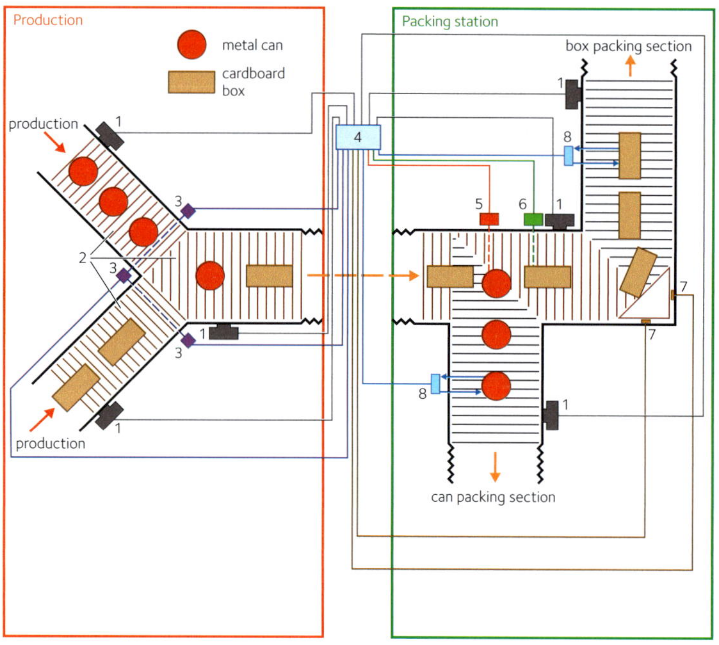


1 ______ 5 ______
2 ______ 6 ______
3 ______ 7 ______
4 ______ 8 ______

★★★ c) Complete the definitions with words from the text.

1 In a modern factory conveyor belts are controlled by ______.
2 A ______ proximity sensor reacts to light.
3 An ______ proximity sensor only reacts to metals.
4 A ______ proximity sensor can recognize cardboard.
5 A ______ switch reacts if it is touched.
6 An ______ sensor uses sound waves.

Modern manufacturing processes use programmable logic controllers (PLCs) to regulate material flow. In the diagrams above, the PLC controls the speed at which metal cans and cardboard boxes from the production hall of a factory are transported on conveyor belts to the packing station. The PLC's job is to control the six electric motors which drive the belts and it does this by using data from different types of sensors. When the cans and boxes leave production, they first pass through two photoelectric proximity sensors which stop and start the belts to make sure there is enough room for the objects on the next belt. When the metal cans and cardboard boxes reach the packing station, an inductive proximity sensor recognizes the metal in the cans and activates a belt to transport them to the can packing section. Next a capacitive proximity sensor detects the non-conductive cardboard and switches on the belt to the box packing section. If too many card-board boxes build up, they press against the triangular corner piece. This activates one or both of the two limit switches which react to direct pressure and switch off the belt so the blockage can be cleared. Finally, ultrasonic sensors are used to count the cans and boxes.

21

## 2 A guided tour of a factory

A guide is explaining how sensors are used in his food-processing factory.

★ a) Listen and say which three of the following statements are false.

| | | T | F |
|---|---|---|---|
| 1 | Mike begins by showing them a video. | | |
| 2 | The canning machine is operated by robots. | | |
| 3 | The sensor for the soup-canning machinery uses sound waves. | | |
| 4 | The conveyor belt has the same type of sensor as the canning machinery. | | |
| 5 | The sensor for the roll of plastic film is like the one for the conveyor belt. | | |
| 6 | They finish the tour by having a meal in the canteen. | | |

★★ b) Correct the three false statements.

1 ____________________

2 ____________________

3 ____________________

★★★ c) Write these expressions from the recording under the four headings. There are three for each heading.

Here you can see how … • I very much hope you enjoyed it. • If you'd like any more information, I'll be pleased to help. • I'll be your guide this morning. • I'm going to start with … • My name's … • Our next stop is … • The … (e.g. sensor) consists of … • Now the next thing I want to show you is … • Well, we've come to the end of our tour … • … (e.g. "PLC") stands for … • Good morning and welcome to …

| Greeting the visitors | Structuring the tour | Explaining | Finishing the tour |
|---|---|---|---|
| | | | |

**IT'S YOUR TURN**

A group of English-speaking visitors is coming to visit your workplace. Use the role cards below to prepare a guided tour. Act out the situation in front of the other members of your class.

| Guide |
|---|
| Good … and welcome to … |
| My name is / Our names are … |
| Before we start, we'd like to give each of you a name tag / brochure / … |
| The toilets/restrooms are … |
| We're going to start with a video/… |
| We'll start the tour at/in the … |
| We'll walk from here to the … |
| Please follow me/us. |
| Please be careful. |
| Please don't touch the … |
| Would anyone like a coffee/poster/…? |
| Are there any questions? |

| Visitor |
|---|
| Excuse me, is there a toilet/restroom …? |
| Could you explain what a/an … is, please? |
| What does this thing/device/… do? |
| I'd/We'd like to know more about the …? |
| How does this work? |
| How many people work here? |
| Who is responsible for …? |
| Do you have a quality control department / …? |
| Is it always this noisy/quiet/clean/dirty/…? |
| How many … do you produce a day / …? |
| We're especially interested in … |
| I'm sorry, I didn't catch that. Can you repeat that, please? |

# Extra practice: Units 17–20

## 1 Electrical symbols

★ a) How many symbols can you label? Label as many as possible before looking for them in units 17 and 18.

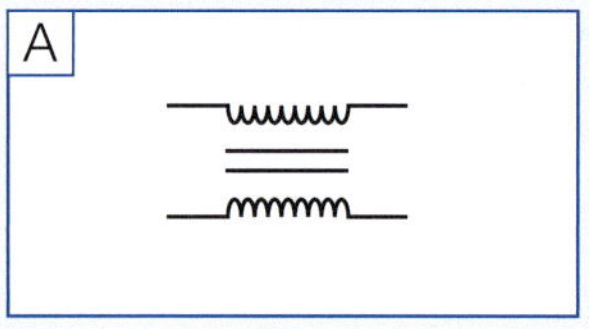


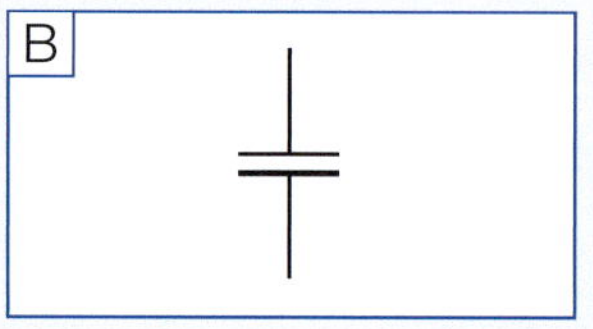


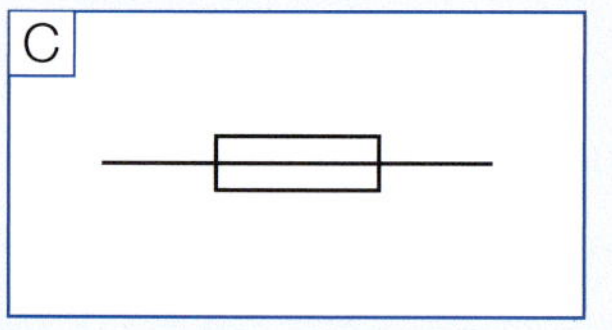


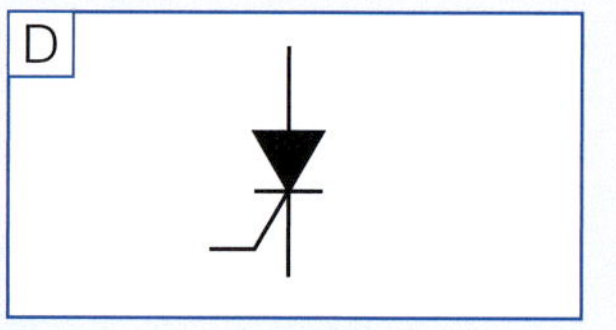


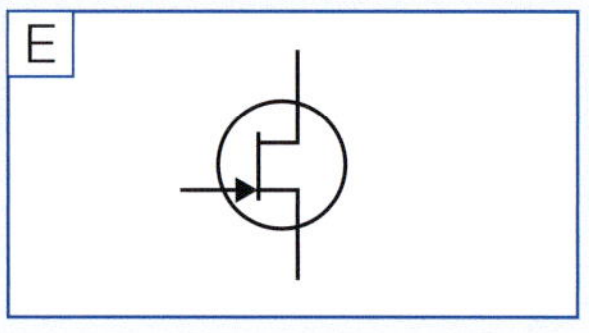


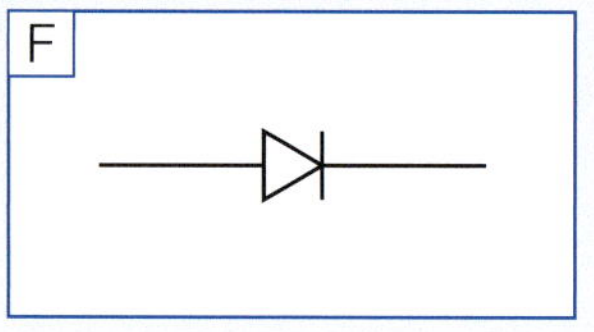


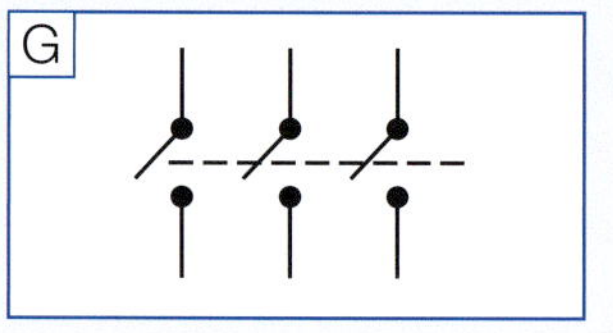


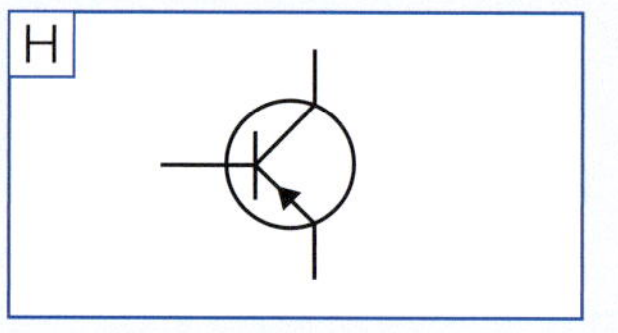


★★ b) Match each definition with one or more of the symbols above.

1 It protects an electric circuit against an overcurrent.
2 It steps a current up or down.
3 It stores an electric charge.
4 It uses a magnetic field produced by a low current to switch on a more powerful current.
5 It uses two or more p-n junctions to make a low current control, switch or amplify a stronger one.

1 ____ 2 ____ 3 ____ 4 ____ 5 ____

★★★ c) Write your own definitions of the symbols not defined in exercise b).

______________________________

______________________________

## 2 Bimetallic thermostat

An electrician should know about bimetallic thermostats.

★ a) Use the words in the box to label points 1–6 of the diagram.

brass • bimetallic strip • closed • current • gap • iron

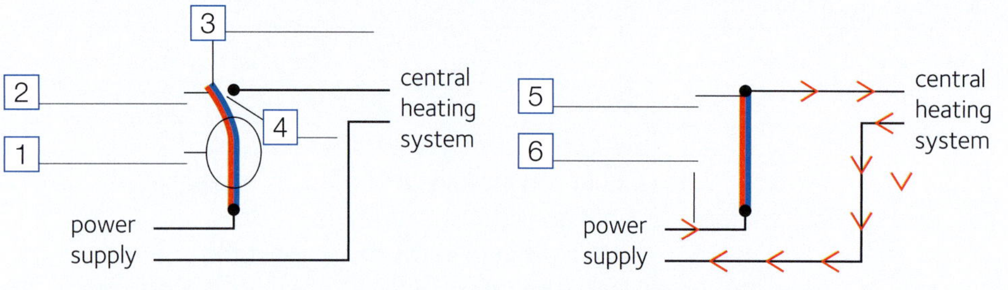


**Tip**

Iron expands less than brass as it gets hotter.

| | |
|---|---|
| biegen | bend |

★★ b) Explain how the thermostat works in a few sentences.

______________________________

______________________________

______________________________

______________________________

______________________________

22

## 3 A guided tour of a modern warehouse

You are going to listen to a guided tour of a factory that uses many electronic devices.

★ a) Listen to the tour and complete the sentences with a), b) or c).

| 1 | Fabian Schilling's company |
|---|---|
| a | sells goods. |
| b | delivers goods. |
| c | buys goods. |

| 2 | The warehouse is open |
|---|---|
| a | all day. |
| b | all night. |
| c | all day and night. |

| 3 | The warehouse has |
|---|---|
| a | no people. |
| b | no vehicles. |
| c | no goods. |

| 4 | An AGV is |
|---|---|
| a | an employee. |
| b | a vehicle. |
| c | an on-board computer. |

| 5 | A PLC is |
|---|---|
| a | an employee. |
| b | a vehicle. |
| c | an on-board computer. |

| 6 | The vehicles in the warehouse are |
|---|---|
| a | driverless. |
| b | petrol-driven. |
| c | noisy. |

| 7 | The vehicles in the warehouse follow routes marked by |
|---|---|
| a | sensors in the floor. |
| b | magnets in the floor. |
| c | magnets and sensors in the floor. |

| 8 | All the goods in the warehouse have |
|---|---|
| a | sensors. |
| b | magnets. |
| c | microchips. |

★★ b) Write a few sentences to explain what an AGV is in more detail.

★★★ c) List the advantages of using AGVs in a warehouse. Can you think of any more? Write them down. Compare them with your neighbour.

## ▶▶▶ ICH KANN

| | Seite/Übung |
|---|---|
| ☐ Ich kann eine eingeübte, kurze und einfache Präsentation zu einem Thema vortragen, das mir vertraut ist. Ich kann dabei einfache Nachfragen beantworten, wenn ich um Wiederholung bitten kann. A2 | 45/It's your turn; 49/It's your turn |
| ☐ Ich kann in einfachen zusammenhängenden Sätzen Diagramme beschreiben und interpretieren. B1 | 45/3; 47/2a |
| ☐ Ich kann eine Rolle in einem Dialog oder einer Simulation übernehmen (z. B. Berufssituation). A2 | 51/ It's your turn |
| ☐ Ich kann kurzen und deutlich gesprochenen Texten und Tonträgern die wesentlichen Informationen entnehmen, wenn es um vorhersehbare alltägliche oder berufsspezifisch vertraute Dinge (z. B. Beschreibung von Elektrizität, Gleichstrom, *Lenz's Law*) geht. A2 | 44/2; 47/3; 47/It's your turn; 51/2a |
| ☐ Ich kann Anweisungen, Fragen und Auskünfte in Alltags-, Ausbildungs- und Berufssituationen im Wesentlichen verstehen. A2 | 45/4a; 49/3 |
| ☐ Ich kann einfachen Alltagstexten, die sich auf vertraute Situationen beziehen, die wichtigsten Informationen entnehmen (z. B. berufliche Alltagsbeschreibungen, Gleich-/Wechselstrom, Sicherheitsbeschreibung). A2 | 44/1a |
| ☐ Ich kann Informationen in verschiedenen längeren Texten oder Textteilen finden, die ich brauche, um eine bestimmte Aufgabe zu lösen. B1 | 46/1a, b, c |
| ☐ Ich kann Wörter und Sätze richtig abschreiben. A1 | 45/4b; 47/2b; 49/1c; 51/2c |

# 21 Talking to colleagues

**This unit is about:**
- company hierarchy
- polite language
- small talk

**Competences:**
- treating colleagues with respect
- using polite forms
- making small talk

## 1 Talking to colleagues

As an apprentice you will come into contact with many different people at all levels in your company from both Germany and abroad. When talking to them, it is important to remember their status and expectations. Match the people (1–5) with the descriptions (A–E).

1 A master electrician
2 An Irish work placement student
3 A newly qualified electrician
4 The human resources manager
5 The managing director

A has files on all the company's employees and their performance.
B remembers very well how it feels to be an apprentice.
C hopes to learn about the job and enjoy a few weeks in Germany.
D is the most powerful person in the company.
E trains the apprentices and expects them to follow instructions.

## 2 Professional behaviour

It is always important to be polite. Look at the following examples of polite and impolite language.

| Polite | Impolite |
|---|---|
| Could you possibly be a little quieter, please? | Be quiet! |
| Would you just pass me the multimeter, please? | Pass me the multimeter. |
| I'm afraid we're very busy at the moment. | We're busy. Go away! |
| Would it be possible to come back in an hour? | Come back later. |
| Would you mind waiting? | Wait here. |

The following sentences are taken from conversations between colleagues at work.

★ a) Compare the following sentences with the examples above. Mark the polite sentences with a "p" and the impolite sentences with an "i".

☐ "I can't hear what you're saying over the noise of the machine, so be quiet."
☐ "Would you mind waiting for a few minutes?"
☐ "I hope you're happy with the result."
☐ "Give me the screwdriver."
☐ "It's our lunch break. Go away!"
☐ "I'm afraid my boss has just left. Can I help you?"

★★ b) Underline the words that make the sentences sound polite.

★★★ c) Write polite versions of the three impolite sentences in exercise a).

______________________________

______________________________

______________________________

23 🎧 3

## Chatting to a colleague on a building site

Angela from Edinburgh has just started working on a big building site in Vienna for a month. On Friday afternoon she meets another worker called Anton, who has just finished his apprenticeship at a local company.

★ a) Listen to the dialogue and fill in the gaps.

Angela: Hello, I don't think I've seen you here before.

Anton: No, that's because I've just started work here. My name's Anton. I'm a ____________ 1.

Angela: Nice to meet you, Anton. I've just started here, too. My name's Angela. I'm an ____________ 2. I'm from Edinburgh. Where are you from?

Anton: I'm from Vienna.

Angela: That's great! Perhaps you can tell me something about the city.

Anton: Well, we have ____________ 3 and ____________ 4 and, of course, the famous Viennese ____________ 5 that all the tourists know about. But there's also the Naschmarkt.

Angela: I'm afraid I didn't quite catch that. The …?

Anton: The Naschmarkt. We call it Vienna's great stomach. It's the city's most famous ____________ 6. It's a great place to go at the weekend. You can buy ____________ 7, ____________ 8 and ____________ 9 there.

Angela: I'm afraid I don't really like cooking …

Anton: But there are also lots of marvellous ____________ 10 and ____________ 11 in Vienna, too.

Angela: Now that sounds interesting!

Anton: And every Saturday there's a big ____________ 12.

Angela: That's tomorrow! Perhaps we can go there together, if you have time.

Anton: Yes, fine. You can come with me tomorrow morning. I'm going shopping there with my ____________ 13.

★★ b) Work with a partner. Read the dialogue again and then practise acting it out from memory. Take it in turns to play each role.

**IT'S YOUR TURN**

Imagine you have an English-speaking work placement student at your company. Work with a partner and make a list of the interesting things to see and do where you live or nearby and then act out a role-play with the visitor like the one above. Use the phrase box.

| | |
|---|---|
| Are you interested in… (e.g. art, culture, music, sport, shopping, sightseeing, nature)? | I'm (not) very interested in … |
| When are you free? | I'm free in the evenings / at weekends / on Saturday. |
| When do you finish work on … (e.g. Friday)? | I finish work at … (e.g. about 4 o'clock). |
| What are you doing … (e.g. tomorrow evening)? | I'm not doing anything / I'm meeting … in a pub/bar. |
| Would you prefer to … or …? | I'd prefer to … (e.g. go to a football match). / I don't mind. |
| How about … (e.g. going to a football match)? | Yes, that's a great idea! / I'd love to do that! |

# 22 Dealing with customers

**This unit is about:**
- code of conduct
- being polite
- customer feedback

**Competences:**
- understanding and applying a code of conduct
- listening to a dialogue with a customer
- interacting with customers

## 1 How to deal with customers

The Electrical Services' code of conduct gives employees helpful suggestions when dealing with customers. Read the extract below.

- Be polite and professional at all times.
- Arrive at the site a few minutes before the time agreed with the customer.
- Be smartly dressed in our company's uniform.
- Always give the customer your full attention.
- Make sure you fully understand what the customer requires.
- Handle the customer's property with care and respect.
- Invite the customer to give feedback on the quality of your work.
- Take any criticism and/or complaints extremely seriously.

★ a) Complete the sentences below with a), b) or c).

1 Employees should arrive on the site
a) at exactly the agreed time b) earlier than the agreed time c) soon after the agreed time.
2 On the site employees must wear
a) their own clean clothes b) fashionable clothes c) company clothing.
3 If your mobile rings when you are talking to a customer, you must
a) ignore it b) say sorry to the customer and answer it c) ask the customer if you can answer it.
4 If you move a customer's furniture in order to do a job in a house, you should then
a) explain to the customer why you moved it b) put it back where it was c) leave the house quietly.
5 When you finish a job, you should
a) leave the site quickly b) tell the customer you are leaving c) ask if the customer is satisfied with your work.
6 If you receive negative customer feedback when you have finished a job, you should
a) listen carefully and try to find a solution b) tell them to contact your boss c) promise to tell your boss.

★★ b) Work with a partner and think of the best thing to do in the following situations.

1 You are a qualified electrician working with an apprentice in a private house. At 2 p.m. on a Friday afternoon you tell the apprentice to check the basement and bring up the tools while you bring round the van. The student brings the tools, you load everything into the van and the apprentice goes home by public transport. Suddenly the owner of the house comes up to you and tells you angrily that you have left a mess in his basement. You check it and see a pile of old cables and electrical fittings left in a heap on the floor. You have a company mobile and the apprentice's mobile phone number. What is the best solution in this situation?

2 One day your boss gives you three jobs to do, and you see that the first one is in a jeweller's shop. You have to be there by 8 a.m. in order to repair the alarm system before the shop opens at 9.00 a.m. The owner, who lives 30 km away, will leave home early and unlock the shop for you. You drive to the shop in a company van using the satnav, but get stuck in a traffic jam. Finally, when the traffic clears, the satnav says you won't be at the shop until 8.45. Your next job is at an office block near the jeweller's and you have to be there by 9.30 a.m. at the latest. You phone the jeweller on your mobile. What do you say to him?

★★★ c) Choose one of the two situations above and role-play a dialogue between yourself and the angry customer in which you find a solution to the problem. Use the phrase box at the end of this unit and make sure you are polite and professional.

24 

## 2 Talking to customers

You are an apprentice electrician. You and a qualified colleague have just finished doing some work in an international footballer's luxury penthouse in the city centre. Before you leave you ask Marilyn Trump, his personal assistant, if she is satisfied with the work.

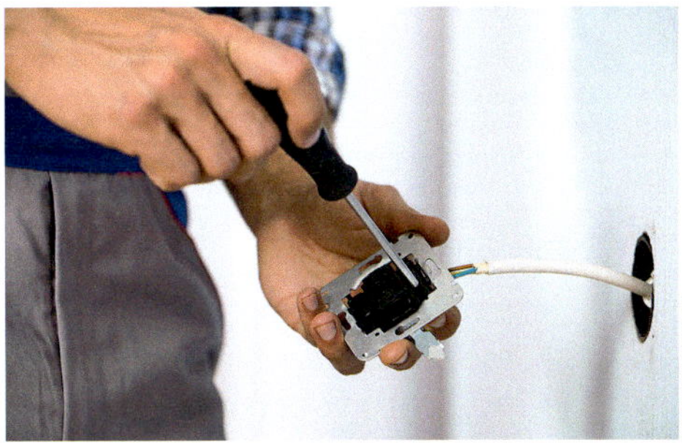
Fotolia.com/Andrey Popov

★ a) Work with a partner and underline the three impolite answers the electrician gives to the customer.

Electrician: We've finished now, Miss Trump. Would you like to take a look at what we've done?
PA: I just hope it's perfect because Mr Looney can get very angry!
Electrician: I'm sure everything is fine, Miss Trump. Here in the bedroom we've put in some new sockets for …
PA: Look at the floor! It's covered in mud from your shoes! And there's a piece of wire next to the sockets!
Electrician: The mud's from Shane Looney's football boots! That's not our fault. We can take the wire, but the mud's your problem. Clean it up yourself.
PA: What other work have you done?
Electrician: In the recreation room we've put in two extra sockets for his electric train set and …
PA: Only two? He told me he wanted four extra sockets, two for the train set and two for his electronic drum kit.
Electrician: Our instructions say two sockets not four. Contact the company if you want more sockets.
PA: What other work have you done?
Electrician: We've also put in a socket for the electronic punch bag. The socket's fine but the machine doesn't work.
PA: Doesn't work? In that case you must have played with it and broken it! It was fine this morning. I heard Mr Looney using it.
Electrician: No, no, he must have broken it himself. The machine's your problem, Miss Trump, not ours. Buy a new one. He has enough money.

★★ b) Re-write the three impolite parts of the dialogue in a more polite form. Use the phrase box.

______________________________________________

______________________________________________

______________________________________________

★★★ c) Listen to the recording of the dialogue and compare your polite sentences with what you hear. Which is better? Now work with a partner and take it in turns to act out each of the two roles from memory.

| Sympathy and apologies | Offering a solution | Polite phrases |
|---|---|---|
| I see what you mean. | We'll … (e.g. clean up / repair the machine / change the installation). | No problem, … (name). |
| I see your point. | We can send someone to … (e.g. check/repair/replace the …). | I'm sure we can … (e.g. help you / find a solution). |
| I fully understand. | It'll only take a minute to … (e.g. fix it). | Is there anything else we can do for you? |
| I/We apologize for the mistake/misunderstanding. | | |

**IT'S YOUR TURN**

The Electrical Services' code of conduct is used in your company. Write down the three most important points in order of importance. Compare your results with a partner. Talk about your own experiences and agree on the two most important points. Then have a class discussion.

# 23 Job advertisements

**This unit is about:**
- job advertisements
- recruitment agencies
- application documents

**Competences:**
- understanding a job advertisement
- planning a job application
- comparing options

## 1 Working in another continent

Frank Hinz and his classmates are almost at the end of their apprenticeships at Electro Terminal in Kassel and some of them plan to work abroad. They find the following website on the Internet.

★ a) Read the text and match the words in blue with their German equivalents in the box.

☐ Begleitschreiben • ☐ Betreffzeile • ☐ Arbeitgeber • ☐ Lebenslauf (*AE*) • ☐ Personal • ☐ Personalvermittler • ☐ Pflichtfelder • ☐ zurzeit

| Jobcom Human Resources[1] Services |
|---|
| Fast Growing City Dubai & Abu Dhabi<br>Currently[2] recruiting onshore and offshore electricians. We have a network of thousands of recruiters[3], human resources managers and company directors in Dubai and Abu Dhabi. |
| **Upload CV/résumé** |
| Compulsory fields[4] are marked with an asterisk*.<br>Upload the CV/résumé[5] you would like to send to recruiters and employers[6].<br>*Click "Browse" to locate your CV/résumé on your computer ______________ Browse<br>*Enter a title for your CV/résumé: ______________ |
| **Covering letter[7]** |
| *Covering letter subject line[8] ______________<br>(This subject line will appear in all correspondence with employers.)<br>*Copy and paste your covering letter in this box. ☐ |

★★ b) Study the advertisement and choose the correct statements.

| 1 | This advert was placed by |
|---|---|
| a | an oil company. |
| b | the cities of Dubai and Abu Dhabi. |
| c | a recruitment agency. |

| 2 | An HR manager works with |
|---|---|
| a | people. |
| b | electricity. |
| c | oil. |

| 3 | To get a job with this company you need to supply |
|---|---|
| a | one document. |
| b | two documents. |
| c | three documents. |

| 4 | A CV or résumé has details of |
|---|---|
| a | the jobs you want. |
| b | the training you want. |
| c | your education, training and skills. |

★★★ c) Write a few sentences to describe what sort of company Jobcom is and how it works.

______________________________________________

______________________________________________

## 2 Working closer to home

The next website that Frank and his classmates look at has an advertisement for a job in the UK.

★ a) Study the advertisement and find the English equivalents of these German words.

| | | | |
|---|---|---|---|
| 1 | verlängerbar ______ | 2 | so bald wie möglich ______ |
| 3 | Elektroinstallationsfirma ______ | 4 | Aufgaben ______ |
| 5 | Wartung ______ | 6 | Leerrohr ______ |
| 7 | Leitungsführung ______ | 8 | (Kabel)träger ______ |
| 9 | Sicherungstafel ______ | 10 | Renovierung ______ |

INSTALLATION ELECTRICIAN

| | |
|---|---|
| Pay rate: | £16/hour minimum |
| Location: | Colchester, Essex, UK |
| Job type: | 2 to 4-month contract, renewable, some overtime available |
| Starting date: | ASAP |
| Contact: | Mike Soames, Powerserve Global Recruitment, PO Box 999, London SW1 4HX, United Kingdom |

JOB DESCRIPTION

Our client is an electrical contractor working in schools, colleges, leisure centres, libraries and office buildings. The duties will involve installation, maintenance, conduit, cable trunking and tray work and will also include light fittings, fuse boards and electrical refurbishment.

WHO SHOULD APPLY?

You are a qualified electrician interested in working on commercial or industrial electrical systems. You are hard-working with a professional attitude and good communication skills.

Register online and upload your CV **HERE** →

★★ b) Read the job advertisement and say

- where the job is.
- how long you can work there.
- how much you can earn.
- the opportunities for overtime.
- whether an electrical contractor or a recruitment agency is advertising this job.

★★★ c) Study the advertisement and write your own description of the sort of person the company is looking for and where he or she will be working.

______

______

**IT'S YOUR TURN**

You are thinking about applying for a new job. Why would you or would you not apply for this job? Use the phrase box.

| |
|---|
| I've always wanted to … (e.g. travel, see another country/continent, work abroad). |
| The job would give me the chance to … (use my skills / learn new skills / improve my English / see the world). |
| I have a good job offer … (from my employer / another company / in my home town). |
| I want to live … (at home / near home / with my girlfriend/boyfriend). |
| My parents want me to … (live nearby / take over the family business / travel the world). |

# 24 Job applications

**This unit is about:**
- curriculum vitae (*BE*) / résumé (*AE*)
- covering letters
- job interviews

**Competences:**
- writing a CV/résumé
- writing a covering letter / cover letter
- handling a telephone interview

## 1 Curriculum vitae (CV)

Frank Hinz decides to apply for the job in Dubai / Abu Dhabi advertised by Jobcom in unit 23 (see page 58). He finds out that an English CV is different from a German "Lebenslauf" and adapts his to fit the job advertisement. Work with a partner or in small groups and do the following tasks.

**Tip**
Always adapt your CV to fit the job advertisement. Don't use the same CV again and again!

★ a) List what Frank leaves out in the English version of his CV.

★★ b) List the headings in Frank's CV that are not normally found in a German CV.

★★★ c) List any other differences and discuss possible reasons for these differences with your partner/group.

**Frank Hinz**
Goethestraße 44, 34119 Kassel, Germany
Landline[1]: +49 561 757366, Mobile: +49 176 6338452
Email: frank.hinz@linkall.de

**PROFILE**[2]
Newly qualified electrician seeking post abroad.
Good[3] spoken and written English. Mobile and flexible.

**KEY SKILLS**
– Electrical installation in private, commercial and industrial buildings
– Specialist knowledge of security systems

**PROFESSIONAL TRAINING**
2011–2015 4-year apprenticeship at Electro Terminal & Co and the Hesse[4] Vocational Training College for Electrical Engineering in Kassel, Germany.

**EDUCATION**
2001–2011 Primary and secondary education in Kassel[5]

**WORK EXPERIENCE**
2010 5-day placement at Elektro Fischer (local electrical contractor) doing maintenance and repairs of industrial wiring

**RELEVANT SKILLS**[6]
Full driving licence
First aid certificate
Life-saving certificate

**EXTRA-CURRICULAR ACTIVITIES**[7]
Voluntary member of Hesse Rescue Service
Captain of local soccer team
Active member of church community service group

**PERSONAL DETAILS**
Date of birth: 10 February[8] 1995
Nationality: German

**Erläuterungen**
1 Das Pluszeichen ersetzt den Auslandscode 00.
2 Hier erfährt der/die Arbeitgeber/in auf einen Blick, wer der/die Bewerber/in ist und was er/sie kann.
3 Die Beherrschung einer Fremdsprache wird mit *fluent*, *good* und *basic* beschrieben.
4 Alle deutschen Begriffe (z. B. Berufsschule) sind ins Englische zu übersetzen.
5 Eine knappe Bezeichnung der schulischen Laufbahn reicht für eine handwerkliche Tätigkeit.
6 Alle weiteren für das Arbeiten im Ausland relevanten Fähigkeiten sind hier zu erwähnen.
7 Alle außerschulischen Aktivitäten, die Aufschluss über die Persönlichkeit des Bewerbers / der Bewerberin geben, sind anzugeben.
8 Monate immer ausschreiben.

## 2 Planning your CV

You decide to apply for a job abroad and start preparing your CV. Match the information below with suitable headings from Frank Hinz's CV.

| Information | Heading |
|---|---|
| 1 Highly motivated and hard-working | |
| 2 Sound engineer for rock band | |
| 3 Week's work placement with local electrical contractor | |
| 4 Motorcycle licence | |
| 5 Automation and process control technology | |

## 3 Writing a covering letter

Michael Althoff applies for a job as an electrician with Outriggers International and contacts Bill Ridges in Human Resources. Use words from the box to fill in the gaps in his covering letter.

apprenticeship • available • cables • experience • interested • licensed • motivated • notice • offshore • position

Dear Mr Ridges

I am very ____________________ [1] in working as an electrician in the ____________________ [2] drilling industry.

By July 20.. I will have completed my 4-year ____________________ [3] at Heller Starkstromtechnik GmbH in Passau and will then be a ____________________ [4] electrician. I have ____________________ [5] in installing and maintaining overhead power ____________________ [6] for trams in Hungary, Slovakia and the Czech Republic.

My English is good and I am highly ____________________ [7] and flexible.

I am ____________________ [8] for an interview at short ____________________ [9] in person or on the telephone and very much hope you will consider me for this ____________________ [10].

Yours sincerely

Michael Althoff

25

## 4 Job interview

You want to improve your job interview skills.

★ a) Listen to the telephone interview with Bill Ridges and Michael Althoff and complete the sentences.

1 Bill Ridges wants to ask Michael ____________________.
2 Michael works on ____________________.
3 Bill Ridges wants to know something about ____________________.
4 Michael is prepared to be away from home on an oil rig for ____________________.
5 Michael can't think of ____________________.
6 Bill Ridges is going to send Michael ____________________.

★★ b) Explain why you think Michael has made a good or bad impression on Bill Ridges.

**IT'S YOUR TURN**

You want to apply for a job abroad. Apply for one of the jobs on pages 58 or 59. Use the examples in this unit to write your CV and covering letter. Make sure you adapt your CV to fit the job.

# Extra practice: Units 21–24

## 1 Role-play

You register with an international online recruitment agency specializing in jobs for electricians and phone their hotline to ask for advice with your application.
Act out the following dialogue with a partner and then swap roles.

| Recruitment agent | You |
| --- | --- |
| Good morning and thank you for calling Electrical Recruitment International. You're through to Jackie Miller. How can I help you? | Geben Sie Ihren vollen Namen an und erklären Sie, dass Sie einen Job im Ausland suchen. |
| Could you tell me a little more about yourself, Mr/Ms …? | Erklären Sie, dass Sie … Jahre alt sind und in … wohnen. Sie haben Ihre Ausbildung im … (Monat/Jahr) abgeschlossen und suchen eine Stelle in … (Ort im Ausland) oder … als Elektriker/in. |
| What skills do you have? | Beschreiben Sie Ihre Fähigkeiten und eventuellen Schwerpunkte. |
| Why do you want to work abroad and not in Germany? | Begründen Sie in ein paar Sätzen Ihren Wunsch, im Ausland zu arbeiten. |
| What other countries have you been to with your school or on holiday? | Beschreiben Sie Ihre Auslandsaufenthalte und schildern Sie, welche Erfahrungen Sie mit Ihren Englischkenntnissen gemacht haben. |
| What sort of a person are you? How would your employer and teachers describe you? | Stellen Sie sich vor, wie Ihr/e Arbeitgeber/in und Ihre Berufsschullehrer/innen Sie beschreiben würden. |
| Do you have any questions you would like me to answer? | Denken Sie sich zwei oder drei Fragen aus. |

## 2 Dealing with customers

You have just completed a job in the offices of an international law firm, so before you leave you ask the office manager to check your work.

★ a) Work with a partner and underline the impolite sections of the dialogue.

**Electrician:** We've finished now, Mrs Buffett. Would you like to see what we've done and then sign the acceptance form?
**Office manager:** Yes, certainly.
**Electrician:** In office no. 1 we've disconnected the central light and put it up in the corner, as requested.
**Office manager:** Oh dear! Now it's very dark. I think it was better where it was!
**Electrician:** Bad luck. You wanted it in the corner and that's where it is.
**Office manager:** Is it too late to put it back where it was?
**Electrician:** Contact the office and tell them you made a mistake. I have no time to change it now.
**Office manager:** What other work have you done?
**Electrician:** Please come this way to office no. 2. Here, we've installed the data projector on the ceiling, as instructed. You can switch it on and off with the remote control.
**Office manager:** Oh no! You've attached the black data projector! Everything else in this room is white! It doesn't match the colour scheme. We wanted the white data projector on the ceiling.
**Electrician:** What's the difference? No one looks at the ceiling anyway. Your colleague told us where to find the projector and we found this one. Your colleague made the mistake, not us. If you want a white one on the ceiling, you can put it there yourself. Anyone can do a job like that.
**Office manager:** What other work have you done?
**Electrician:** That's it. Sign here.

★★ b) Use the polite phrases at the end of unit 24 to re-phrase the four impolite sentences.

★★★ c) Practise performing the dialogue with a partner then perform it in front of the class *from memory* or with the help of the following prompts:

| | |
|---|---|
| Electrician: | Central light – corner |
| Senior clerk: | Oh no! … |
| Electrician: | Suggests solution |
| Senior clerk: | Reacts to solution |
| Electrician: | Black data projector – ceiling |
| Senior clerk: | Oh no! … |
| Electrician: | Suggests solution |
| Senior clerk: | Reacts to solution – polite ending |
| Electrician: | Polite ending |

## ▶▶▶ ICH KANN

| | Seite/Übung |
|---|---|
| ☐ Ich kann meine Meinung, Pläne, Absichten und Ziele darlegen und einfach begründen. B1 | 59/ It's your turn |
| ☐ Ich kann eine Rolle in einem Dialog oder einer Simulation übernehmen (z. B. Berufssituation). A2 | 55/3b; 55/It's your turn; 56/1c; 57/2c |
| ☐ Ich kann kurzen und deutlich gesprochenen Texten und Tonträgern die wesentlichen Informationen entnehmen, wenn es um vorhersehbare alltägliche oder berufsspezifisch vertraute Dinge (z. B. Beschreibung von Elektrizität, Gleichstrom, *Lenz's Law*) geht. A2 | 55/3a; 57/2c; 61/4 |
| ☐ Ich kann einfachen Alltagstexten, die sich auf vertraute Situationen beziehen, die wichtigsten Informationen entnehmen (z. B. berufliche Alltagsbeschreibungen, Gleich-/Wechselstrom, Sicherheitsbeschreibung). A2 | 54/1; 54/2a, b; 57/2a |
| ☐ Ich kann Informationen in verschiedenen längeren Texten oder Textteilen finden, die ich brauche, um eine bestimmte Aufgabe zu lösen. B1 | 56/1a; 58/1a, b; 61/2a, b |
| ☐ Ich kann Listen schreiben und einfache Formulare ausfüllen. A1 | 60/1a, b, c |
| ☐ Ich kann Wörter und Sätze richtig abschreiben. A1 | 59/It's your turn; 61/3 |
| ☐ Ich kann einen kurzen, einfachen Text über ein persönliches Erlebnis oder eine Erfahrung (z. B. Ausbildung, Beruf) schreiben. A2 | 54/2c; 58/1c, 59/2c |
| ☐ Ich kann einen einfachen Lebenslauf und ein einfaches Bewerbungsschreiben verfassen. B1 | 61/ It's your turn |

# Wordlist

## A

| | |
|---|---|
| to accelerate | *beschleunigen* |
| accumulator | *Akku(mulator)* |
| acid | *Säure* |
| acid paste | *Säurepaste* |
| to activate | *aktivieren* |
| advantage | *Vorteil* |
| adventure | *Abenteuer* |
| advert | *Inserat, Anzeige* |
| advice | *Rat, Ratschlag* |
| to advise | *beraten* |
| to affect | *betreffen* |
| air conditioner | *Klimaanlage* |
| air shaft | *Luftschacht* |
| alarm | *Alarmanlage; alarmieren* |
| alternating current | *Wechselstrom* |
| ammeter | *Strommesser* |
| amount | *Menge* |
| to amplify | *verstärken* |
| amusement park | *Vergnügungspark* |
| angle grinder | *Winkelschleifer* |
| anode | *Anode, positiver Pol* |
| antenna | *Antenne* |
| apart | *auseinander* |
| appliance | *Gerät, Anwendung* |
| application | *Ver-, Anwendung* |
| application (for a job) | *Bewerbung (um eine Stelle)* |
| to apply (voltage) | *(Spannung) anlegen* |
| to apply for a job | *sich um eine Stelle bewerben* |
| apprentice | *Auszubildende/r* |
| approximately | *ungefähr, circa* |
| armature | *Armatur, Anker* |
| art gallery | *Kunstgalerie* |
| to assume | *annehmen, davon ausgehen* |
| atomic particle | *Atomteilchen* |
| to attach to | *verbinden mit* |
| to attract | *(sich) anziehen (Wirkung)* |
| automation | *Automatisierung* |
| available | *erhältlich, verfügbar* |
| average | *Durchschnitt; durchschnittlich* |
| axle | *Achse* |

## B

| | |
|---|---|
| bare wire | *blanker Draht* |
| battery | *Batterie* |
| battery charger | *Batterieaufladegerät* |
| battery pack | *Akku(mulator)* |
| belt (conveyor) | *Band* |
| belt sander | *Schwingschleifer* |
| to bend open | *aufbiegen* |
| bimetallic strip | *Bimetallstreifen* |
| bipolar junction transistor | *zweipoliger Schicht-transistor* |
| blackout | *Stromausfall* |
| blade fuse | *Sicherung mit Messer-kontakten* |
| block of wood | *Holzblock, -klotz* |
| to block sth | *etw blockieren, absperren* |
| blocking | *Blockieren, Sperren* |
| to blow a fuse | *durchbrennen* |
| bolt of lightning | *Blitzstrahl* |
| to boost | *erhöhen, verstärken* |
| brake | *Bremse* |
| brass | *Messing* |
| bridge rectifier | *Brückengleichrichter* |
| bright | *hell* |
| brush (contact) | *(Kontakt-)Bürste, Stromabnehmer* |
| building site | *Baustelle* |
| buried cable | *unterirdisches Kabel* |
| button cell | *Knopfzelle* |

## C

| | |
|---|---|
| cab | *Taxi* |
| cable | *Kabel* |
| cable trunking | *Leitungsführung* |
| to calculate | *berechnen* |
| calculator | *Taschenrechner* |
| called, to be | *heißen* |
| camera flash unit | *Blitzgerät* |
| can | *Dose, Büchse* |
| to cancel out | *aufheben* |
| canning machinery | *Füllanlage* |
| capacitance | *Kapazität* |
| capacitive proximity sensor | *kapazitiver Näherungs-sensor* |
| capacitor | *Kondensator* |
| car aerial | *Autoantenne* |
| car dashboard | *Armaturenbrett* |
| car relay | *Autorelais* |
| car seat-positioning motor | *Motor zur Sitz-verstellung* |
| carbon | *Kohlenstoff* |
| cardboard | *Pappe* |
| cartridge fuse | *Patronensicherung* |
| casing | *Gehäuse* |
| to catch | *etw. mitbekommen (hören)* |
| to catch fire | *Feuer fangen, in Brand geraten* |
| cathode | *Kathode, negativer Pol* |
| ceiling | *Decke* |
| central heating | *Zentralheizung* |
| CFL (compact fluorescent lamp) | *Energiesparlampe* |
| chain reaction | *Kettenreaktion* |
| to change | *ändern, wechseln* |
| change gear | *in einen anderen Gang schalten* |
| channel | *Kanal* |
| to charge | *(auf)laden (von Akkumulatoren, Kondensatoren)* |
| charged particles | *geladene Teilchen* |
| chart | *Diagramm, Tabelle* |
| to check | *kontrollieren* |
| chemical reaction | *chemische Reaktion* |
| to choose | *wählen* |
| circle | *Kreis* |
| circuit | *Schaltung, Kreislauf, (Strom-)Kreis* |
| circuit breaker | *Leitungsschutzschalter* |
| circular movement | *Kreisbewegung* |
| closed loop control | *geschlossener Regel-kreis* |
| clutch | *Kupplung* |
| coal-fired | *mit Kohlefeuerung* |
| to coat | *beschichten, belegen* |
| coil | *Windung, Spule, Spirale* |
| colleague | *Kollege/Kollegin* |
| collision | *Zusammenstoß, Kollision* |
| colour rendition | *Farbwiedergabe* |
| commercial | *handelsüblich* |
| common contact | *gemeinsamer Kontakt* |
| commonly used | *oft/typisch verwendet* |
| community service | *gemeinnützige Tätig-keit, Zivildienst* |
| commutator | *Kollektor, Stromwender* |
| complicated | *kompliziert* |
| component | *Bauteil* |
| compressed air | *Druckluft* |
| compressor | *Kompressor* |
| condition | *Zustand* |
| conductor | *Leiter* |
| conduit | *Kabelrohr* |
| to connect (to) | *(miteinander) verbin-den, anschließen* |
| to consist of | *bestehen aus* |
| consumer | *Verbraucher/in, Konsument/in* |
| consumer unit | *Verbrauchereinheit* |
| consumption | *Verbrauch* |
| contactor | *Schütz* |
| continuous action controller | *kontinuierliche Regeleinrichtung* |
| continuously | *kontinuierlich* |
| to contract | *(sich) zusammenziehen* |
| contractor | *Unternehmer (mit Werkvertrag)* |
| to control | *steuern, regeln* |
| control circuit | *Steuerkreis* |
| conveyor belt | *Fließ-, Förderband* |
| cooker | *(Elektro-)Herd* |
| copper | *Kupfer; kupfern* |
| copper wire | *Kupferdraht* |
| cordless drill | *Akku-Schrauber, -Bohrer* |
| core | *Kern* |
| correspondence | *Briefwechsel, Korrespondenz* |
| cosmetic use | *kosmetische Verwendung* |
| to count | *zählen* |
| cover(ing) letter | *Begleitschreiben, -brief* |
| crossword (puzzle) | *Kreuzworträtsel* |
| cruise control | *Tempomat* |
| crystal earpiece | *Kristallhörer* |
| current | *Strom, Strömung* |
| curriculum vitae / résumé | *Lebenslauf* |
| customer | *Kunde/Kundin* |

## D

| | |
|---|---|
| to damage | *beschädigen* |
| dangerous | *gefährlich* |
| data projector | *Beamer* |
| dead (battery) | *leer* |
| decoration | *Dekoration* |
| deep-sea diving | *Tiefseetauchen* |
| defined as | *definiert als* |
| to deliver | *liefern* |
| to demonstrate | *demonstrieren, zeigen* |
| depending on | *hängt ab von, je nachdem* |
| desired | *gewünscht* |
| destination | *Ziel, Bestimmungsort* |
| device | *Vorrichtung, Gerät, Apparat* |
| dimmable | *dimmbar* |
| diode | *Diode* |
| direct current | *Gleichstrom* |
| direction | *Richtung* |
| disadvantage | *Nachteil* |
| to disconnect | *trennen, herausziehen* |
| discontinuous action controller | *unterbrochene Regel-einrichtung* |
| dishwasher | *Geschirrspüler* |
| to divert | *ablenken* |
| divided by | *geteilt durch* |
| divorced | *geschieden* |

| | |
|---|---|
| drill | *Bohrer, Bohrmaschine; bohren* |
| drilling industry | *Ölbohrindustrie* |
| driverless | *führerlos* |
| to drop | *fallen lassen* |
| dry cell battery | *Trockenbatterie* |
| duty | *Pflicht* |
| dynamo | *Lichtmaschine, Dynamo* |

## E

| | |
|---|---|
| earth | *Erde, Masse* |
| earth-moving machinery | *Erdbaumaschinen, Großgerät* |
| economical | *wirtschaftlich* |
| efficiency | *Wirkungsgrad* |
| efficient | *effizient, wirksam* |
| electric charge | *elektrische Ladung* |
| electric cooker | *Elektroherd* |
| electric fan | *elektrischer Ventilator* |
| electric generator | *Stromgenerator* |
| electric heater | *Elektroheizung, elektrisches Heizgerät* |
| electric iron | *elektrisches Bügeleisen* |
| electric jigsaw | *elektrische Stichsäge* |
| electrical contractor | *Elektroinstallateur* |
| electrical engineer | *Elektroingenieur/in* |
| electrician | *Elektriker/in* |
| electricity | *Elektrizität, Strom* |
| electrocardiograph | *Elektrokardiograph* |
| electromagnetic | *elektromagnetisch* |
| electron | *Elektron* |
| electronic | *elektronisch* |
| element | *Element* |
| emission | *Emission, Ausstoß, Abgase* |
| to emit | *emittieren, ausstoßen* |
| employer | *Arbeitgeber/in* |
| encoder | *Kodiergerät, Impulsgeber* |
| to energize | *aufladen* |
| energy | *Energie* |
| energy-efficient | *energiesparend* |
| energy monitoring | *Energiekontrolle* |
| to enter (current) | *(Strom) einfließen* |
| environment | *Umwelt* |
| to equal | *gleich sein* |
| equation | *Gleichung* |
| equipment | *Geräte, Maschinen* |
| everywhere | *überall* |
| estimate | *Kostenvoranschlag* |
| to examine | *untersuchen* |
| to expel | *ausstoßen* |
| expensive | *teuer* |
| experience | *(Berufs-)Erfahrung* |
| experiment | *Versuch, Experiment; experimentieren* |
| explanation | *Erklärung* |
| to explode | *explodieren* |
| expression | *Ausdruck* |
| extension reel | *Verlängerungskabel* |
| external | *Außen-, von außen* |
| extra-curricular activity | *außerschulische Aktivität* |
| extractor fan | *Entlüfter, Abzugshaube* |

## F

| | |
|---|---|
| factor | *Faktor* |
| factual mistake | *Sachfehler* |
| to fail | *versagen, ausfallen* |
| fan | *Ventilator, Lüfter* |
| to fasten (seatbelt) | *sich anschnallen* |
| fault | *Fehler* |
| faulty | *fehlerhaft, defekt* |
| feedback | *Rückmeldung* |
| field coil | *Feldspule* |
| field-effect transistor | *Feldeffekt-Transistor* |
| filament | *(Glüh-)Faden* |
| file | *Akte, Ordner* |
| film projector | *Filmprojektor* |
| fire and rescue service | *Feuerwehr- und Rettungsdienst* |
| fittings | *Zubehör, Verschraubungen* |
| flexible | *flexibel* |
| floodlight | *Flutlicht* |
| to flow | *fließen; Durchlauf, Bewegung* |
| fluorescent tube | *Leuchtröhre* |
| fog light | *Nebelscheinwerfer* |
| force | *Kraft* |
| foreman | *Vorarbeiter/in* |
| fork-lift truck | *Gabelstapler* |
| four squared | *vier hoch zwei, vier im Quadrat* |
| fraction of a second | *Bruchteil einer Sekunde* |
| frequency | *Frequenz* |
| friction | *Reibung* |
| fridge | *Kühlschrank* |
| fuel | *Brenn-, Kraft-, Treibstoff* |
| fuel consumption | *Kraftstoffverbrauch* |
| full driving licence | *Führerschein aller Klassen* |
| fuse | *Sicherung* |
| fuse box/board | *Sicherungskasten* |

## G

| | |
|---|---|
| gap | *Lücke* |
| gasoline | *Benzin* |
| gearbox | *Getriebe* |
| gearwheel | *Getrieberad* |
| gender | *Geschlecht* |
| to generate | *erzeugen* |
| generator | *Generator* |
| ghost | *Geist* |
| glass vial | *Glasfläschchen, -ampulle* |
| to glow | *glühen* |
| graph | *Kurve, Grafik* |
| gravity | *Erdanziehungskraft* |
| to grease | *schmieren* |
| grid | *Gitter* |
| ground/earth | *Erde* |

## H

| | |
|---|---|
| hairdryer | *Fön* |
| halogen lamp | *Halogenlampe* |
| handbook | *Bedienungsanleitung, Handbuch* |
| to happen | *passieren, geschehen* |
| to harm | *verletzen, beschädigen* |
| headlights | *Scheinwerfer* |
| heater | *Heizgerät* |
| heavy goods vehicle driving licence | *Lkw-Führerschein* |
| heavy metal | *Schwermetall* |
| hedge trimmer | *Heckenschere* |
| highlighted | *hervorgehoben* |
| high-tension cable | *Hochspannungskabel* |
| high-voltage | *Hochspannungs-* |
| to hit | *schlagen, gegen etwas kommen* |
| holder | *Halter(ung)* |
| home charging station | *Ladestation für zu Hause* |
| household | *Haushalt; Haushalts-* |
| householder | *Hauseigentümer/in* |
| huge | *riesig* |
| human resources | *Personal(abteilung), Mitarbeiter/in* |
| hybrid vehicle | *Hybridfahrzeug* |
| hydroelectric power station | *Wasserkraftwerk* |

## I

| | |
|---|---|
| impolite | *unhöflich* |
| incandescent bulb | *Glühbirne* |
| to increase | *erhöhen* |
| indefinitely | *unbestimmt* |
| to induce | *auslösen* |
| inductive proximity sensor | *induktiver Näherungssensor* |
| inefficient | *ineffizient, unwirtschaftlich* |
| inert gas | *Edelgas* |
| inexact | *ungenau* |
| inlet valve | *Einlassventil* |
| to insert | *einführen* |
| to install | *installieren, einrichten* |
| installation | *Installation, Anlage* |
| instructor | *Ausbilder/in* |
| instructions | *Anweisungen, Anleitungen* |
| insulation | *Isolierung* |
| intense | *intensiv* |
| internal combustion engine (ICE) | *Verbrennungsmotor* |
| to interpret | *dolmetschen* |
| invisible | *unsichtbar* |
| iron | *Eisen; Bügeleisen* |

## J

| | |
|---|---|
| joined | *verbunden* |
| journey | *Fahrt* |
| junction | *Kreuzung* |

## K

| | |
|---|---|
| to keep clear | *freihalten* |
| to kick in | *einsetzen, sich einschalten* |
| to kill | *töten* |
| knife | *Messer* |

## L

| | |
|---|---|
| to label | *beschriften, benennen; Etikett* |
| laboratory | *Labor(atorium)* |
| lamp | *Lampe, Leuchte* |
| layer | *Schicht* |
| lead | *Blei* |
| lead dioxide | *Bleidioxid* |
| lethal | *tödlich* |
| lever | *Hebel* |
| licensed | *genehmigt, amtlich zugelassen* |
| to lift | *heben* |
| light | *Licht, Lampe, Leuchte; erleuchten* |
| light bulb | *Glühbirne* |
| light fittings | *Beleuchtungskörper, Beleuchtungszubehör* |
| lightning | *Blitz* |
| lightning strike | *Blitzschlag* |
| to limit | *begrenzen* |
| limit switch | *End(ab)schalter, Begrenzungsschalter* |
| limited | *beschränkt, begrenzt* |
| liquid | *Flüssigkeit* |
| lithium-ion battery | *Lithium-Ionen-Batterie* |
| live (circuit) | *stromführend (Stromkreis)* |
| load | *Ladung, Last, Belastung; belasten, laden* |
| to locate | *platzieren, laden* |
| to lock | *(ab)schließen* |
| long(est) lasting | *langdauernd, am längsten haltend* |

| | |
|---|---|
| loop control system | *Regelkreissystem* |
| looter | *Plünderer/in* |
| to lose | *verlieren* |
| low | *niedrig* |
| to lower | *verringern; niedrig* |

**M**

| | |
|---|---|
| magnet | *Magnet* |
| magnetic field | *Magnetfeld* |
| (the) mains | *Stromnetz* |
| to maintain | *warten, instandhalten* |
| maintenance | *Wartung, Instandhaltung* |
| majority | *Mehrzahl* |
| manufacturer | *Hersteller/in* |
| marital status | *Familienstand* |
| married | *verheiratet* |
| mathematical signs | *mathematische Zeichen* |
| to measure | *messen* |
| medical use | *medizinische Verwendung* |
| to mention | *erwähnen* |
| mercury | *Quecksilber* |
| misconception | *Missverständnis* |
| mobile | *mobil, beweglich* |
| mobile phone | *Mobiltelefon, Handy* |
| motivated | *motiviert* |
| motorway | *Autobahn* |
| movable contact | *beweglicher Kontakt* |
| movement | *Bewegung* |
| MRI scanner | *Kernspintomograph* |
| multi-coloured | *mehrfarbig, vielfarbig* |
| multimeter | *Vielfachmessinstrument* |

**N**

| | |
|---|---|
| nail | *Nagel* |
| name tag | *Namensschild* |
| necessary | *nötig* |
| to need | *brauchen* |
| negative | *negativ* |
| neighbour | *Nachbar(in)* |
| neutrons | *Neutronen* |
| nickel | *Nickel* |
| nickel-metal hydride battery | *Nickel-(Metallhydrid)-Batterie* |
| nitrogen | *Stickstoff* |
| noise | *Geräusch* |
| noisy | *laut* |
| nought | *Null* |

**O**

| | |
|---|---|
| to observe | *beachten* |
| office block | *Bürogebäude, -hochhaus* |
| off-peak electricity | *Strom außerhalb der Stoßzeiten* |
| oil rig | *Ölplattform* |
| open loop control | *offener Regelkreis* |
| to operate | *an-, betreiben* |
| to oppose | *sich widersetzen* |
| opposite | *gegensätzlich* |
| opposites | *Gegensätze* |
| outside | *außerhalb* |
| overalls | *Overall, Arbeitsanzug* |
| overcurrent | *Überstrom* |
| overhead cable | *Überlandleitung* |
| to overheat | *(sich) überhitzen* |
| to overload | *überlasten* |

**P**

| | |
|---|---|
| packing station | *Packstation* |
| painter | *Maler/in, Anstreicher/in* |
| panel | *Anzeige-, Schalttafel* |
| paper clip | *Büroklammer* |
| parallel, in parallel | *parallel geschaltet* |
| to pass through | *durchfließen* |
| performance | *Leistung* |
| period of time | *Zeitraum, -spanne, -abschnitt* |
| permanent magnet | *permanenter Magnet* |
| petrol engine | *Benzin-, Vergasermotor* |
| petrol station | *Tankstelle* |
| phase | *Phase* |
| photovoltaic cell | *photoelektrische Zelle* |
| physicist | *Physiker/in* |
| pin | *Pol, Kontakt* |
| placement | *Stelle, Anstellung, Praktikum* |
| plastic film | *Plastikfolie* |
| plastic tube | *Kunststoffrohr* |
| plate | *Platte* |
| plug | *Stecker* |
| to plug in | *einstöpseln, anschließen* |
| polarity | *Polarität* |
| pole | *Pol* |
| polite | *höflich* |
| to pollute | *verschmutzen* |
| point | *Punkt; Komma (bei Dezimalzahlen)* |
| positive | *Positivpotential* |
| positive difference | *Spannungsdifferenz* |
| power | *Kraft, Energie, Strom; antreiben* |
| power company | *Stromunternehmen* |
| power consumption | *Stromverbrauch* |
| power cord | *Netz-, Stromkabel* |
| power cut | *Stromausfall, -abschaltung* |
| power distribution | *Stromlieferung* |
| power drill | *elektrische Bohrmaschine, Elektrobohrer* |
| powerful | *leistungsstark; wichtig* |
| power grid | *Strom(versorgungs)netz* |
| power line | *Hochspannungsleitung* |
| power measuring meter | *Stromzähler* |
| power source | *Strom-, Energiequelle* |
| power station | *Kraftwerk* |
| power tool | *Elektrowerkzeug, -gerät* |
| practice | *Übung* |
| to practise | *üben* |
| precaution | *Vorsichtsmaßnahme* |
| presentation | *Vorstellung, Präsentation* |
| pressure | *Druck* |
| to prevent | *verhindern* |
| primary education | *Grundschul(aus)bildung* |
| primary power | *Primärenergie* |
| principle | *Prinzip* |
| to produce | *produzieren, erzeugen* |
| production hall | *Produktionshalle* |
| program switch | *Programmschalter* |
| programmable logic controller (PLC) | *speicherprogrammierbare Steuerung* |
| properties | *Eigenschaften* |
| to protect | *schützen, sichern* |
| protection | *Schutz* |
| proton | *Proton* |
| pylon | *Mast* |
| pub | *Kneipe* |
| purpose | *Zweck, Ziel* |
| push button switch | *Druckschalter* |
| pylon | *Mast* |

**Q**

| | |
|---|---|
| qualified | *qualifiziert, ausgebildet* |
| quality control department | *Qualitätskontrollabteilung* |
| quiet | *leise* |

**R**

| | |
|---|---|
| radio signal | *Funksignal* |
| range | *Radius, Reichweite* |
| RCD (residual current device) | *Fehlerstromschutzschalter, FI-Schalter* |
| to reach | *erreichen* |
| reaction | *Reaktion* |
| to receive | *empfangen* |
| to recharge | *aufladen* |
| rechargeable batteries | *aufladbare Batterien* |
| recording | *Aufnahme* |
| recruiter | *Anwerber/in* |
| recruiting | *Anwerbung* |
| recruitment agency | *Stellen-, Arbeitsvermittlung* |
| to rectify | *berichtigen, gleichrichten* |
| rectifying | *Gleichrichten* |
| to reduce (to) | *reduzieren (auf)* |
| refurbishment | *Renovierung* |
| regenerative braking | *regeneratives Bremsen* |
| to register | *registrieren* |
| to regulate | *regulieren, regeln* |
| relay | *Relais* |
| to release | *freisetzen, -geben* |
| to remember | *sich erinnern* |
| remotely | *ferngesteuert* |
| renewable | *erneuerbar; verlängerbar* |
| repairing | *Reparieren* |
| to repel | *abstoßen* |
| to replace | *ersetzen* |
| reservoir | *Stausee, -becken* |
| to reset | *zurückstellen* |
| residential area | *Wohngegend* |
| resistance | *Widerstand* |
| resistor | *Widerstand* |
| restroom *(AE)* | *Toilette, Bad* |
| résumé *(AE)* | *Lebenslauf* |
| to retain | *speichern, behalten* |
| to retrofit | *nachrüsten* |
| to reverse | *rückgängig machen, umdrehen* |
| to revise | *wiederholen* |
| rewirable fuse | *reparierbare Sicherung (in Deutschland unbekannt, war in GB üblich)* |
| ring circuit | *ringförmige Stromverteilung* |
| rod | *Stab* |
| roof | *Dach* |
| to rotate | *rotieren (lassen), drehen* |
| rotation | *Drehung* |
| rotor | *Rotor* |
| to rub | *reiben* |
| rubber band | *Gummiband* |
| rule | *Regel, Vorschrift* |

**S**

| | |
|---|---|
| safety | *Sicherheit* |
| safety device | *Sicherheitsvorrichtung* |
| safety features | *Sicherheitsvorkehrungen, -merkmale* |
| to sand away | *abschleifen, abisolieren* |
| sandpaper | *Sandpapier* |
| satisfied | *zufrieden* |
| satnav | *Navi* |
| to save lives | *Leben retten* |
| schematic | *schematische Darstellung, Grafik* |
| school leaving certificate | *(Schul-)Abschlusszeugnis* |
| scientist | *(Natur-)Wissenschaftler/in* |
| seat | *Sitz* |
| seat belt | *Sicherheitsgurt* |

| | |
|---|---|
| secondary education | *Sekundarstufe I und II* |
| security system | *Sicherheitssystem* |
| semiconductor | *Halbleiter* |
| sensitive | *empfindlich* |
| sensor | *Sensor, (Mess-)Fühler* |
| to separate | *trennen* |
| series, in series | *in Reihe geschaltet* |
| to share | *teilen* |
| to shine (brightly) | *glühen (hell)* |
| shock | *Schlag; schockieren* |
| shop sign | *Ladenschild* |
| to short-circuit | *kurzschließen* |
| shower | *Dusche; duschen* |
| sign | *Schild; unterschreiben* |
| silicon | *Silizium* |
| site (building site) | *Baustelle* |
| skill | *Fertigkeit, Fähigkeit* |
| slow; to slow (down) | *langsam; verlangsamen* |
| smell of burning | *Brandgeruch* |
| smoke detector | *Rauchmelder* |
| smoothly | *ebenmäßig* |
| socket | *Steckdose* |
| sodium lamp | *Natriumlampe* |
| solar panel | *Solarkollektor* |
| solar power | *Solarenergie* |
| solution | *Lösung* |
| sometimes | *manchmal* |
| sound | *Laut, Ton* |
| sound engineer | *Toningenieur/in* |
| source | *Quelle* |
| spark | *Funke* |
| spark plug | *Zündkerze* |
| specifications | *(technische) Angaben* |
| speed | *Geschwindigkeit* |
| speed control unit | *Radarkontrolle, Blitzgerät* |
| to spend (money) | *(Geld) ausgeben* |
| to spin | *(sich) (schnell) drehen* |
| split-ring commutator | *Stromwender (mit Stromwender-lamellen)* |
| sports stadium | *(Sport-)Stadion* |
| spring | *Feder* |
| spur (circuit) | *Stromkreis, Stromkreis-abzweigung, Spur* |
| square root | *Quadratwurzel* |
| squared | *zum Quadrat* |
| squirrel-cage rotor | *Käfiganker* |
| stale | *abgestanden* |
| statement | *Aussage* |
| stationary | *stehend, im Stand* |
| stationary contact | *feststehender Kontakt* |
| stator | *Ständer* |
| steam | *Dampf* |
| to step up/down | *hoch/heruntertrans-formieren* |
| storage power plant | *Speicherwasser-kraftwerk* |
| store | *Vorrat; speichern* |
| storeroom | *Lagerraum* |
| strength | *Stärke* |
| structure of the atom | *Atomstruktur* |
| subject line | *Betreffzeile* |
| substation | *Umspannwerk* |
| to suck in | *einsaugen* |
| to suggest | *vorschlagen* |
| suitable | *geeignet, passend* |
| suited to | *geeignet für* |
| sulphuric acid | *Schwefelsäure* |
| summary | *Zusammenfassung* |
| supercapacitor | *Superkondensator* |
| supplier | *Anbieter/in, Lieferant/in* |
| to supply | *liefern; Lieferung* |
| to surprise | *überraschen* |
| survey | *Umfrage, Untersu-chung; untersuchen* |
| switch (on/off) | *Schalter; (um)schalten (an/aus)* |
| switchboard | *Satzbautafel* |
| switched fused connection | *Schaltsicherung* |
| switchgear | *Schaltgerät, -vorrichtung* |
| to switch | *(um-)schalten* |
| switching unit | *(Um-)Schaltgerät* |
| symbol | *Symbol, Zeichen* |

## T

| | |
|---|---|
| table | *Tabelle* |
| to tag | *kennzeichnen* |
| to tape to | *kleben an* |
| technical drawing | *technische Zeichnung* |
| technician | *Techniker/in* |
| temperature | *Temperatur* |
| terminal | *Ausgang, Anschluss* |
| thought | *Gedanke* |
| three-phase induction motor | *Drehstrom(induktions) motor* |
| throttle | *Drossel(klappe), drosseln* |
| thyristor | *Thyristor* |
| to and fro | *hin und her* |
| toggle switch | *Kippschalter* |
| top rates | *Spitzenlöhne, -gehälter* |
| torch | *Taschenlampe* |
| torque | *Drehmoment, -kraft* |
| to touch | *anfassen* |
| touch, to be in touch | *sich melden* |
| tough | *hart, rau* |
| traditional | *traditionell* |
| traffic lights | *(Verkehrs-)Ampel* |
| trainee | *Auszubildende/r, Praktikant/in* |
| traineeship | *Ausbildung(sverhältnis), Lehre* |
| training | *Ausbildung, Schulung* |
| tram | *Straßenbahn* |
| to transform | *umwandeln* |
| transformer | *Transformator* |
| transmission line | *Übertragungsleitung* |
| to transmit | *übertragen* |
| tray work | *Kabelträger* |
| triangular | *dreieckig* |
| to trip sth | *etw aktivieren* |
| troubleshooting | *Fehlersuche* |
| tube | *Rohr* |
| tumble dryer | *Trommeltrockner* |
| tungsten | *Wolfram* |
| turbine | *Turbine* |
| turn | *sich drehen* |
| turns of wire | *Drahtwindungen* |

## U

| | |
|---|---|
| ultrasonic sensor | *Ultraschallschalter* |
| underground cable | *unterirdisches Kabel* |
| undersea cable | *Seekabel* |
| to unlock | *aufschließen* |
| upper | *höhere(r, -s)* |

## V

| | |
|---|---|
| value | *Wert* |
| valve | *Ventil* |
| variable capacitor | *Drehkondensator* |
| variable frequency drive (VFD) | *Antrieb mit Frequenz-umrichter* |
| vehicle | *Fahrzeug* |
| ventilation system | *Belüftungssystem* |
| vessel | *Behälter* |
| vial | *Fläschchen* |
| video camera | *Videokamera* |
| visible | *sichtbar* |
| voltage | *Spannung* |
| voltage regulator | *Spannungsregler* |
| voluntary member | *freiwilliges Mitglied* |

## W

| | |
|---|---|
| warehouse | *Lager(halle)* |
| warning | *Warnung* |
| washing machine | *Waschmaschine* |
| waste | *Verschwendung; verschwenden* |
| water-cooled | *wassergekühlt* |
| wattage | *Wattleistung* |
| weak point which breaks first | *Sollbruchstelle* |
| to wear out | *abnutzen, verschleißen* |
| wheel | *Rad* |
| wind turbine | *Windkraftrad, Wind-turbine* |
| windings | *Windungen* |
| wire | *Draht, Kabel* |
| wiring system | *Verkabelung* |
| wooden base | *Holzplatte* |
| to work out | *ausrechnen, heraus-finden* |
| work placement | *Praktikum* |
| work properly | *richtig funktionieren* |
| workmate | *Kollege/in* |
| workshop | *Werkstatt, Werkshalle* |
| wound in loops | *spiralförmig gewickelt* |
| to wrap (around) | *binden, umwickeln* |
| wristwatch | *Armbanduhr* |

## X

| | |
|---|---|
| xenon short arc lamp | *Xenon-Kurzlichtbogen-lampe* |
| X-ray machine | *Röntgengerät* |

## Z

| | |
|---|---|
| Zener diode | *Zener-Diode* |
| zinc | *Zink* |

# JOB MATTERS
## ELEKTROTECHNIK


| | |
|---|---|
| Verfasser: | Michael Benford, Wolf-Rainer Windisch |
| Projektleitung: | Kerstin Adlesgruber, Simone Conrad |
| Verlagsredaktion: | Verena Reiter, Kari-ann Warnakulasuriya |
| Redaktionelle Mitarbeit: | Christine House |
| Umschlaggestaltung: | vitaledesign, Berlin |
| Layout: | Julia Dresch, Alois Kandler |
| Technische Umsetzung: | Breiner Satzstudio; Oxana Rödel, Absatz DTP-Service, Teltow |
| Coverfoto: | Shutterstock / gyn9037 |
| Illustrationen: | Oxford Designers & Illustrators |

Erhältlich sind auch:

| | |
|---|---|
| Handreichungen für den Unterricht als Download | ISBN 978-3-06-451328-0 |
| Audios als Download | ISBN 978-3-06-451329-7 |


Soweit in diesem Lehrwerk Personen fotografisch abgebildet sind und ihnen von der Redaktion fiktive Namen, Berufe, Dialoge und Ähnliches zugeordnet oder diese Personen in bestimmte Kontexte gesetzt werden, dienen diese Zuordnungen und Darstellungen ausschließlich der Veranschaulichung und dem besseren Verständnis des Inhalts.

www.cornelsen.de

Die Webseiten Dritter, deren Internetadressen in diesem Lehrwerk angegeben sind, wurden vor Drucklegung sorgfältig geprüft. Der Verlag übernimmt keine Gewähr für die Aktualität und den Inhalt dieser Seiten oder solcher, die mit ihnen verlinkt sind.


1. Auflage, 1. Druck 2016

Alle Drucke dieser Auflage sind inhaltlich unverändert und können im Unterricht nebeneinander verwendet werden.





Druck: H. Heenemann, Berlin

ISBN 978-3-06-451327-3

PEFC/04-31-1156

PEFC zertifiziert
Dieses Produkt stammt aus nachhaltig bewirtschafteten Wäldern und kontrollierten Quellen.
www.pefc.de